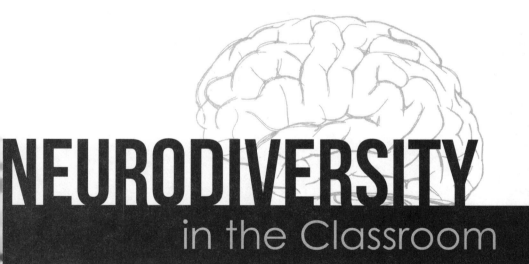

NEURODIVERSITY
in the Classroom

ASCD MEMBER BOOK

Many ASCD members received this book as a
member benefit upon its initial release.

Learn more at: **www.ascd.org/memberbooks**

Thomas
ARMSTRONG

NEURODIVERSITY
in the Classroom

Strength-Based Strategies

to Help Students with Special Needs

Succeed in School and Life

 Alexandria, VA USA

1703 N. Beauregard St. • Alexandria, VA 22311 1714 USA
Phone: 800-933-2723 or 703-578-9600 • Fax: 703-575-5400
Website: www.ascd.org • E-mail: member@ascd.org
Author guidelines: www.ascd.org/write

Gene R. Carter, *Executive Director;* Mary Catherine (MC) Desrosiers, *Chief Program Development Officer;* Richard Papale, *Publisher;* Genny Ostertag, *Acquisitions Editor;* Julie Houtz, *Director, Book Editing & Production;* Ernesto Yermoli, *Editor;* Lindsey Smith, *Graphic Designer;* Mike Kalyan, *Production Manager;* Keith Demmons, *Desktop Publishing Specialist;* Andrea Wilson, *Production Specialist*

ASCD Member Book, No. FY13-1 (Dec. 2012, P). ASCD Member Books mail to Premium (P), Select (S), and Institutional Plus (I+) members on this schedule: Jan., PSI+; Feb., P; Apr., PSI+; May, P; July, PSI+; Aug., P; Sept., PSI+; Nov., PSI+; Dec., P. Select membership was formerly known as Comprehensive membership.

PAPERBACK ISBN: 978-1-4166-1483-8   ASCD product #113017
Also available as an e-book (see Books in Print for the ISBNs).

Quantity discounts: 10–49 copies, 10%; 50+ copies, 15%; for 1,000 or more copies, call 800-933-2723, ext. 5634, or 703-575-5634. For desk copies: www.ascd.org/deskcopy

Library of Congress Cataloging-in-Publication Data

Armstrong, Thomas, author.
  Neurodiversity in the classroom : strength-based strategies to help students with special needs succeed in school and life / Thomas Armstrong.
    pages cm
  Includes bibliographical references and index.
  ISBN 978-1-4166-1483-8 (pbk.)
  1. Children with disabilities–Education–United States. 2. Special education–United States. I. Title.
  LC4031.A68 2012
  371.9–dc23
                          2012033785

22 21 20 19 18 17 16 15 14 13 12   1 2 3 4 5 6 7 8 9 10 11 12

And what do we teach our children? We teach them that two and two make four, and that Paris is the capital of France. When will we also teach them what they are? We should say to each of them: Do you know what you are? You are a marvel. You are unique. In all the years that have passed, there has never been another child like you. . . . You may become a Shakespeare, a Michelangelo, a Beethoven. You have the capacity for anything. Yes, you are a marvel.

—Pablo Casals

NEURODIVERSITY
in the Classroom

Strength-Based Strategies to Help Students with
Special Needs Succeed in School and Life

Introduction

I remember the day like it was yesterday. I had just been hired for my first teaching job in Montreal, Canada, as a special education teacher. My district supervisor wanted to take me around and show me some model special education programs before I actually began teaching. We entered the first classroom, where there were about 10 students working (or at least sitting) quietly at their desks. They were about 8 or 9 years old. I was especially impressed by how quiet they were—overly quiet, really. The special education teacher welcomed us into her classroom with a broad smile. Then, in a voice loud enough to be heard by all the children, she announced, "These are my *slow* students."

My heart sank and I thought to myself, "Is the teacher insane? Doesn't she realize that these kids have *ears*?" I felt embarrassed standing there, as if I myself was a party to this gross insensitivity.

The moment passed, however, and before long I was taking charge of my own junior high special education classroom. My students were not overly quiet. In fact, I had a knack (some might say a curse) for bringing out in my students whatever shadowy emotions were swirling around just below the surface. Not infrequently, my students would come up to me and ask, "Mr. A., why do we have to be in this *retarded* classroom?" I'd mumble something about their needing extra help and would leave it at that. But I was troubled by the question.

Over the next several years of teaching, I'd be confronted again and again with this basic dilemma. On the one hand, I was providing students with special help to remediate their learning and behavior difficulties, which was good. On the other hand, I was also presiding over a system that segregated these kids based upon their negative attributes, which wasn't so good. As one former special education student, now an adult, told me, "They thought I was bad at something, so they tested me to find exactly how bad I was at it, and then spent the next years of my life making me do what I was bad at as much as possible."

Take a moment to consider this little thought experiment. Think about your greatest difficulty or limitation in life, whatever that might be (academic or nonacademic). Now imagine that you have been tested and found wanting in that area, and that you are then sent to a special program where you spend most of your time focusing on that area. Not a very pretty picture, is it? Yet this is what many children in special education face on a daily basis.

The history of special education in the United States, of course, presents a more complex picture. Without going into the whole legislative history, suffice it to say that during the 1960s and 1970s, due in large part to concerted parent advocacy efforts, increasing government involvement in education, and the growth of scientific research regarding special needs issues, our public schools underwent a sea change in providing services for kids in special education (Osgood, 2007). A breakthrough was achieved in 1975 with the passage of the Education for All Handicapped Children Act, which mandated that every child with special needs in the public schools receive an appropriate education in the least restrictive environment. I started working as a learning disability specialist in 1976. Since that time, research in genetics, the brain, human development, and related fields has increased exponentially, providing an even greater awareness of the needs of children who have been previously unserved or underserved in special education programs.

In the 1980s and 1990s, children diagnosed with attention deficit hyperactivity disorder (ADHD) and related problems such as oppositional defiant disorder and Tourette syndrome were added to the list of those served. In the past decade, children identified as having one or more of the autistic spectrum disorders have been increasingly identified and served in special education programs. Despite the fact that legislative loopholes, budget problems, and lack of public awareness still prevent many eligible students from receiving the services they deserve, one must stand back and marvel at the progress that has been made in special education since the 1950s, when only a handful of children with particularly severe needs were served in the schools, if they were served at all.

As I look back on these developments in special education, I see that it is far better for a child to have her special learning needs identified and addressed in school rather than to languish unrecognized in a regular classroom or be excluded from school entirely. At the same time, since the very beginning of my involvement in special education, I have been concerned about the negativity inherent in the "disability discourse" that takes place in education when we talk about kids with special needs. I am speaking here of an institutionalized discourse consisting of specific words such as *disability, disorder, deficit,* and *dysfunction* to describe students. In many of my previous writings, I have criticized special education for identifying certain children based on what they *can't* do rather than on what they *can* do (see, for example, Armstrong, 1996, 1997, 2000, 2001). It's interesting to me that kids these days often use the phrase "He *dissed* me!" to indicate that they've just been insulted or disrespected. Isn't it possible that we're doing the same thing, albeit in an institutionalized way, when we identify certain kids in school according to what's *wrong* with them?

About This Book

This book is a practical guide for regular and special educators on taking *strengths* as the starting point when helping students with special needs achieve success in school and life. In Chapter 1, I introduce the idea of *neurodiversity*, a revolutionary new concept in special education that employs a positive "diversity" perspective similar to biodiversity and cultural diversity to replace the current "disability" discourse that prevails in today's educational circles. I discuss how the concept has developed over the past decade, and how it can be useful to teachers and administrators of both general and special education in framing a more positive view of students with special needs. Because neurodiversity is essentially an ecological perspective, I also develop the related concept of *positive niche construction*—that is, the establishment of a favorable environment within which a student with special needs can flourish in school. This concept, taken from the fields of biology and ecology, serves as a more positive and constructive way of talking about the federal mandate that students be placed in the "least restrictive environment." Instead of spending all of our efforts in trying to make students with special needs more like "normal" students, I propose we devote more attention to accepting and celebrating their differences. The final part of Chapter 1 describes seven components for positive niche construction, including

1. A comprehensive assessment of a student's strengths,
2. The use of assistive technologies and Universal Design for Learning methodologies,
3. The provision of enhanced human resources,
4. The implementation of strength-based learning strategies,
5. The envisioning of positive role models,
6. The activation of affirmative career aspirations, and
7. The engineering of appropriate environmental modifications to support the development of neurodiverse students.

This strength-based approach can serve as a new way to enrich the field of differentiated instruction by ensuring that we develop teaching interventions that address what is unique and positive about each individual student.

In Chapters 2 through 6, I apply the concepts of neurodiversity and positive niche construction to the following five special needs categories: learning disabilities, ADD/ADHD, autistic spectrum disorders, intellectual disabilities, and emotional and behavioral disorders. In each of these chapters, I examine research that details the strengths, talents, and abilities of students with these specific special needs and describe how to apply the seven components of positive niche construction for each disability category. In each of these chapters, I also show how positive niche construction aligns with the Common Core State Standards and provide examples of how to teach and assess specific English language arts and mathematics standards for students with different special needs.

In Chapter 7, I relate the idea of identifying strength-based learning to inclusive practices by describing the work of the William W. Henderson Inclusion School in Dorchester, Massachusetts. This school represents an exemplary model of inclusion that utilizes many of the practices discussed in this book. I also explore some of the key features of strength-based schools, including the application of Appreciative Inquiry as a method to help create more positive IEPs and the use of a 165-item Neurodiversity Strengths Checklist that educators can use to ensure that each student's strengths are fully identified and incorporated in a meaningful way into their studies.

It is my hope that this book will help change the conversation about students with special needs from a *disability* discourse to a *diversity* discourse. The years I spent as a special education teacher and as a consultant to schools convinced me that the key to helping children with deficits is to first find out as much as we can about their strengths. As part of my consulting work, I used to go into school districts and ask administrators to give me the cumulative files of their most difficult students. I would then take a yellow marker and highlight all the strengths that I noticed: teachers' comments, test scores, grades, and other positive data. Oftentimes this process would reduce a cumulative file of a hundred or more pages to two or three sheets. I would then distribute these two or three pages to participants at the student's IEP meeting. Upon confronting only positive information about the child, participants in the meeting would begin to remember other positive events and attributes, and this would very often lead them to generate new constructive strategies for helping the student succeed in school.

Ultimately, my wish is that this book will assist you in developing a new appreciation for the positive side of your students with special needs, and inspire you to get to work right away in constructing positive environments within which they can blossom.

1 | Neurodiversity: The New Diversity

Defects, disorders, diseases can play a paradoxical role, by bringing out latent powers, developments, evolutions, forms of life, that might never be seen, or even be imaginable, in their absence.

—Oliver Sacks, neurologist

It was the start of a new school year. Mr. Farmington, a first-year 5th grade teacher, was perusing his roster of incoming students when it hit him like a ton of bricks: In his class this year, he was going to have two students with learning disabilities, one student with ADHD, one with autism, one with Down syndrome, and one with an emotional disorder. In a class of 30 students, this ratio seemed like too much to bear. Inclusion is all well and good, thought Mr. Farmington, but he already had too much to do. Disgruntled, he took his roster and his misgivings to his principal, Ms. Silvers.

"I'm not trained as a special education teacher," he told her. "Who's going to help me with all the problems I'm going to face with these kids?"

Ms. Silvers listened carefully to Mr. Farmington's concerns. She understood where he was coming from. She'd heard complaints like his from teachers before and had often responded by reassigning at least some of the special education kids to other classrooms. But in this case, she decided to handle the situation a little bit differently.

"Bill," she said, "I know that you're thinking about these kids as problems and believe that they're just going to make your year harder. First of all, let me assure you that you're going to get a lot of support from the special education staff. But there's something else I want you to know. What if I were to tell you that these kids have talents and abilities that are going to enhance your classroom, and that even might make your year easier and more enjoyable? One of the boys that we diagnosed as having a learning disability is totally into machines and can fix just about anything mechanical. The child with autism is absolutely obsessed with military battles, which should be an asset in your history lessons. The girl with Down syndrome was reported by her 4th grade teacher to be one of the friendliest kids she'd ever worked with in her 30 years of teaching. And the boy with an emotional disorder happens to be an artist who has exhibited his work at a local art gallery."

"Wow," said Mr. Farmington. "I had no idea. I guess I was just reacting to their labels. Thanks for the heads-up."

Mr. Farmington left the meeting with a new, more positive attitude about his kids with special needs and a greater willingness to give them a chance to succeed in his classroom.

The above scenario may strike some as overly optimistic, but it raises an important question: Is it better to think about students with special needs as liabilities or as assets? If it's better to perceive them as assets, then why aren't we doing a better job of identifying their strengths? Google the phrase "strengths of students in special education," and you're likely to find a wide selection of websites focused on the pros and cons of inclusion and labeling, but practically nothing about the specific strengths of kids in special education.

The truth is that since the beginning of special education in the early 1950s, the conversation about children with special needs has been almost exclusively a *disability discourse*. In one way this makes perfect sense. After all, we're talking about kids who are labeled as special education students precisely because they've had difficulties of one kind or another in the classroom. But if we truly want to help these kids succeed in school and in life, it seems to me that we need to make a comprehensive, all-out inventory of their strengths, interests, and capabilities. To do this, we need a new paradigm that isn't solely based upon deficit, disorder, and dysfunction. Fortunately, a new way of thinking about students with special needs has emerged on the horizon to help us: *neurodiversity*.

Neurodiversity: A Concept Whose Time Has Come

The idea of neurodiversity is really a paradigm shift in how we think about kids in special education. Instead of regarding these students as suffering from deficit, disease, or dysfunction, neurodiversity suggests that we speak about their *strengths*. Neurodiversity urges us to discuss brain diversity using the same kind of discourse that we employ when we talk about biodiversity and cultural diversity. We don't pathologize a calla lily by saying that it has a "petal deficit disorder." We simply appreciate its unique beauty. We don't diagnose individuals who have skin color that is different from our own as suffering from "pigmentation dysfunction." That would be racist. Similarly, we ought not to pathologize children who have different kinds of brains and different ways of thinking and learning.

Although the origins of the neurodiversity movement go back to autism activist Jim Sinclair's 1993 essay "Don't Mourn for Us," the term *neurodiversity* was actually coined in the late 1990s by two individuals: journalist Harvey Blume and autism advocate Judy Singer. Blume wrote in 1998, "Neurodiversity may be every bit as crucial for the human race as biodiversity is for life in general. Who can say what form of wiring will prove best at any given moment? Cybernetics and computer culture, for example, may favor a somewhat autistic cast of mind." In 1999, Singer observed, "For me, the key significance of the 'Autistic Spectrum' lies in its call for and anticipation of a politics of Neurological Diversity, or what I want to call 'Neurodiversity.' The 'Neurologically Different' represent a new addition to the familiar political categories of class/gender/race and will augment the insights of the social model of disability" (p. 64).

According to a widely disseminated definition on the Internet, neurodiversity is "an idea which asserts that atypical (neurodivergent) neurological development is a normal human difference that is to be recognized and respected as any other human variation." The online *Double-Tongued Dictionary* characterizes neurodiversity as "the whole of human mental or psychological neurological structures or behaviors, seen as not necessarily problematic, but as alternate, acceptable forms of human biology" (2004). The term *neurodiversity* has gathered momentum in the autistic community and is spreading beyond it to include groups identified with other disability categories including learning disabilities, intellectual disabilities, ADD/ADHD, and mood disorders (see, for example, Antonetta, 2007; Baker, 2010; Hendrickx, 2010; and Pollock, 2009).

This new term has great appeal because it reflects both the difficulties that neurodiverse people face (including the lack of toleration by so-called "normal" or "neurotypical" individuals) as well as the positive dimensions of their lives. Neurodiversity helps make sense of emerging research in neuroscience and cognitive psychology that reveals much about the positive side of individuals with disabilities. It sheds light on the work of Cambridge University researcher Simon Baron-Cohen, who has investigated how the strengths of individuals with autism relate to systems thinking in fields such as computer programming and mathematics (Baron-Cohen, 2003). It manifests itself in the work of University of Wisconsin and Boston College researchers Katya von Karolyi and Ellen Winner, who have investigated the three-dimensional gifts of people with dyslexia (Karolyi, Winner, Gray, & Sherman, 2003). It shows up in the works of best-selling author and neurologist Oliver Sacks, whose many books of essays chronicle the lives of neurodiverse individuals (a term he doesn't use, but of which I think he would approve) as they experience both the ups and downs of their atypical neurological makeup (Sacks, 1996, 1998, 2008).

We should keep in mind that the term *neurodiversity* is not an attempt to whitewash the suffering undergone by neurodiverse people or to romanticize what many still consider to be terrible afflictions (see Kramer, 2005, for a critique of those who romanticize depression). Rather, neurodiversity seeks to acknowledge the richness and complexity of human nature and of the human brain. The concept of neurodiversity gives us a context for understanding why we are so frequently delighted with Calvin's ADHD behavior in the *Calvin & Hobbes* comic strip, amused by Tony Shalhoub's obsessive-compulsive detective on the TV show *Monk,* and inspired by Russell Crowe's performance as Nobel Prize winner John Nash (who has schizophrenia) in the movie *A Brilliant Mind.*

The implications of neurodiversity for education are enormous. Both regular and special education educators have an opportunity to step out of the box and embrace an entirely new trend in thinking about human diversity. Rather than putting kids into separate disability categories and using outmoded tools and language to work with them, educators can use tools and language inspired by the ecology movement to differentiate learning and help kids succeed in the classroom. Until now, the metaphor most often used to describe the brain has been a computer or some other type of machine. But the human brain isn't hardware or software; it's *wetware.* The more we study the brain, the more we understand that it functions less like a computer and more like an ecosystem. The work of Nobel Prize–winning biologist Gerald Edelman supports this view (see, for example, Edelman, 1987, 1998). Edelman wrote, "The brain is in no sense like any kind of instruction machine, like a computer. Each individual's brain is more like a unique rainforest, teeming with growth, decay, competition, diversity, and selection" (quoted in Cornwell, 2007). In fact, the term *brainforest* may serve as an excellent metaphor when discussing how the brain responds to trauma by redirecting growth along alternative neurological pathways, and in explaining how genetic "flaws" may bring with them advantages as well disadvantages. Disorders such as autism, ADHD, bipolar disorder, and learning disabilities have been in the gene pool for a long time. There must be a reason why they're still there. As we'll see in the course of this book, the work of evolutionary psychologists represents a key component in exploring this fascinating question.

The use of ecological metaphors suggests an approach to teaching as well. After all, regular classroom teachers are far more likely to want a "rare and beautiful flower" in their classroom than a "broken," "damaged," or "problem" child. Just as we accept that individual species of plants have specific environmental needs (e.g., sun, soil, water), we need to understand that neurodiverse children require unique ecological nutrients in order to blossom. Teachers should not seek to "cure," "fix," "repair," "remediate," or even "ameliorate" a child's "disability." In this old model, kids are either made to approximate the norm (especially for national accountability tests) or helped to cope with their differences as best they can (the cliché that students can learn to live successful and productive lives "despite" their "disabilities" comes to mind here). Instead, teachers should seek to discover students' unique requirements for optimal growth, and then implement differentiated strategies to help them bloom.

Positive Niche Construction

In the neurodiversity model, there is no "normal" brain sitting in a vat somewhere at the Smithsonian or National Institutes of Health to which all other brains must be compared. Instead, there are a wide diversity of brains populating this world. The neurodiversity-inspired educator will have a deep respect for each child's unique brain and seek to create the best differentiated learning environment within which it can thrive. This practice of differentiating instruction for the neurodiverse brain will be referred to in the course of this book as *positive niche construction.*

In the field of biology, the term *niche construction* is used to describe an emerging phenomenon in the understanding of human evolution. Since the days of Darwin, scientists have emphasized the importance of *natural selection* in evolution—the process whereby organisms better adapted to their environment tend to survive and produce more offspring. In natural selection, the environment represents a static entity to which a species must either adapt or fail to adapt. In niche construction, however, the species *acts directly upon the environment* to change it, thereby creating more favorable conditions for its survival and the passing on of its genes. Scientists now say that niche construction may be every bit as important for survival as natural selection (Lewontin, 2010; Odling-Smee, Laland, & Feldman, 2003).

We see many examples of niche construction in nature: a beaver building a dam, bees creating a hive, a spider spinning a web, a bird building a nest. All of these creatures are changing their immediate environment in order to ensure their survival. Essentially, they're creating their own version of a "least restrictive environment." In this book, I present seven basic components of positive niche construction to help teachers differentiate instruction for students with special needs (see Figure 1.1).

Strength Awareness

If our only knowledge about students with special needs is limited to the negatives in their lives—low test scores, low grades, negative behavior reports, and deficit-oriented diagnostic labels—then our ability to differentiate learning effectively is significantly restricted.

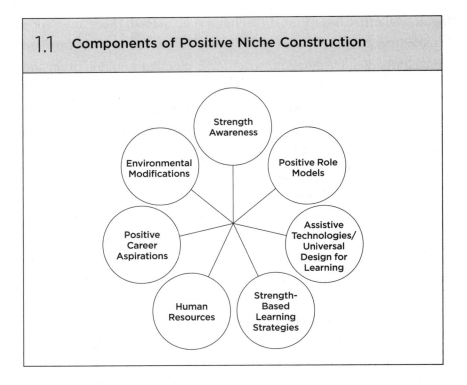

1.1 Components of Positive Niche Construction

Research suggests that teacher expectations powerfully influence student outcomes—a phenomenon that has been variously described as "the Pygmalion effect," "the Hawthorne effect," "the halo effect," and the "placebo effect" (see, for example, Rosenthal & Jacobson, 2003; Weinstein, 2004). As Paugh and Dudley-Marling (2011) note, "'deficit' constructions of learners and learning continue to dominate how students are viewed, how school environments are organized, and how assessment and instruction are implemented" (p. 819).

Perhaps the most important tool we can use to help build a positive niche for the neurodiverse brain is our own rich understanding of each student's strengths. The positive expectations that we carry around with us help to enrich a student's "life space," to use psychologist Kurt Lewin's (1997) term. Educators practicing positive niche construction should become well-versed in a range of strength-based models of learning, including Gardner's theory of multiple intelligences (Armstrong, 2009; Gardner, 1993), the Search Institute's Developmental Assets framework (Benson, 1997), Clifton StrengthsFinder (Gallup Youth Development Specialists, 2007), the Myers-Briggs Type Indicator (Myers, 1995), and Dunn and Dunn's learning style approach (Dunn & Dunn, 1992). Educators ought to know what students in special education are passionate about—what their interests, goals, hopes, and aspirations are. Studies suggest that children who have the capacity to surmount adversity usually have at least one adult in their lives who believes in them and sees the best in them (Brooks & Goldstein, 2001). (See Figure 7.2 in Chapter 7 for a 165-item Neurodiversity Strengths Checklist to use in creating a positive mindset about a student with special needs.)

Example of poor niche construction: Eldon has just been diagnosed as having ADHD and an emotional disorder. In the teacher's lounge, teachers trade stories about his temper tantrums and his failure to comply with school rules. He has been observed commenting to his peers, "I've just been transferred to the retarded class. I guess that means I'm a retard, too." Other students refer to him as a "loser," a "troublemaker," and a "bully."

Example of positive niche construction: Ronell has ADHD and an emotional disorder. He also has been recognized as having leadership capabilities in his gang affiliations, good visual-spatial skills (he enjoys working with his hands), and an interest in hip-hop music. Teachers and students have been instructed to look for Ronell's positive behaviors during the school day and share them with him. Ronell has been informed of his profile of multiple intelligences (high interpersonal, spatial, bodily-kinesthetic, and musical intelligences) and has been observed commenting to his peers, "I guess I'm good at a few things, after all."

Positive Role Models

Children are powerfully influenced by the adults they see in their daily lives. Social learning theory tells us that behavior modeling by adults provides children with one of the major building blocks they require for constructing complex behaviors in life (Bandura, 1986). Scientists suggest that this may be due to the existence of "mirror neurons"—brain cells that fire not only when we do something, but also when we observe others doing that same thing (Rizzolatti & Craighero, 2004).

Adult role models are especially important for kids with special needs. Students with learning disabilities ought to learn about the lives of people who also had learning disabilities and became successful in their chosen careers, such as the novelist John Irving, the actor Whoopi Goldberg, the Nobel Prize–winning biochemist Carol Greider, and the brokerage firm CEO Charles Schwab. Students with ADHD may be heartened to learn about famous people with ADHD, including Olympic athlete Michael Phelps, actor Jim Carrey, film director Stephen Spielberg, and inventor Thomas Edison. Those with intellectual disabilities can take pride in identifying with individuals like them who have accomplished great things, including actor Chris Burke, musician Sujeet Desai, artist Jane Cameron, and college graduate Katie Apostolides. Of course, celebrities aren't the only role models. Neurodiverse adults who have become successful in their local communities should be invited to visit schools, share stories, and provide inspiration for *all* students, not just those with special needs.

Example of poor niche construction: *Susan is a sophomore in high school who has Down syndrome. She has been commenting to her peers and to her teachers that she is "just plain stupid" and that she'd like to drop out of school. One of her teachers calls her "my darling dummy," which elicits laughter from the other students.*

Example of positive niche construction: *Shelly is a freshman in high school who has Down syndrome. Her guidance counselor tells her about Katie Apostolides, a girl with Down syndrome who graduated with an associate's degree from a Pennsylvania college. Now she comments to her teachers, "Maybe I can graduate from high school and go to college like Katie."*

Assistive Technologies and Universal Design for Learning

The vast expansion of emerging technology over the past few decades has provided teachers with many innovative tools for differentiating instruction for students with special needs. These tools allow students to derive knowledge and engage in activities previously inaccessible to them. Assistive technologies cover a wide range of devices and methodologies, including crutches, wheelchairs, grab bars, text telephones, large-print and Braille reading materials, sign language, hearing aids, adaptive keyboards, and augmented and alternative communication devices.

By contrast, the concept of "universal design" was originally developed by urban planners and architects and refers to designs that improve access for people with disabilities while also benefitting the general public (Steinfeld & Maisel, 2012). One of the best illustrations of universal design is the curb cut on a city street. This simple modification not only helps the blind and those in wheelchairs to cross the street more easily, but also benefits joggers, teenagers on skateboards, and parents pushing strollers.

In education, Universal Design for Learning (UDL) refers to the process of removing barriers to learning for kids with disabilities in ways that also enhance everyone else's ability to learn. For example, interactive digital books that provide text, graphics, and speech enable students with learning disabilities to more easily access the printed word while also helping typically developing students become more knowledgeable and productive in their own reading and writing. Universal Design for Learning is based on findings in neuroscience suggesting that there are three primary brain networks (Rose & Meyer, 2002):

- Recognition networks in the posterior areas of the cerebral hemispheres (the "what" of learning),
- Strategic networks in the frontal areas of the cerebral hemispheres (the "how" of learning), and

- Affective networks in the limbic or subcortical areas of the brain (the "why" of learning).

According to the Center for Applied Special Technology (CAST), the UDL framework encourages educators to implement

1. Strategies for presenting information and content to students (recognition networks),
2. Strategies that allow students to express what they know (strategic networks), and
3. Strategies for stimulating and motivating students' interest in learning (affective networks) (CAST Inc., 1999–2012).

The focus of UDL is not strictly on individual students with disabilities (as is the case with assistive technologies), but rather on designing an educational environment that can accommodate a wide range of learning differences. Essentially, assistive technology and UDL represent two approaches that exist along a continuum. As Rose, Hasselbring, Stahl, and Zabala (2005) note, "[a]t the ends of this continuum the two approaches are easily distinguishable. Toward the middle of the continuum, such easy distinctions are muddied, and there are greater points of interaction and commonality" (p. 508).

Example of poor niche construction (without assistive technology): *Sixteen-year-old Samantha has significant intellectual disabilities and gets frustrated when she can't express her needs for food, water, toileting, and other basic necessities. She can easily spiral into tantrums or meltdowns, which often result in some of her favorite activities, such as finger painting and playing with dolls, being taken away from her as part of a behavior modification program. Lately, she has become withdrawn and morose, and an appointment with a psychiatrist has been scheduled.*

Example of positive niche construction (with assistive technology): *Twelve-year-old Irvin has autism and often has difficulty communicating with others. His teacher has purchased the iPad app Proloquo2Go, which Irvin uses to make his needs known. For example, if he's hungry, he simply touches the appropriate button on the screen and a synthesized*

voice says, "I'm hungry." Irvin has discovered that he can now more eas-
ily express his ideas and feelings and has become more communicative.

Example of poor niche construction (without UDL): Ten-year-old
Jason has learning disabilities and struggles with writing. He has begun
to misbehave during writing assignments. He is increasingly spending
writing period in the time-out area and often has to stay in for recess to
make up work.

Example of positive niche construction (with UDL): Eight-year-
old Nathan has learning disabilities and struggles with reading and writ-
ing assignments. His teacher has started using speech-to-text software
with him, which allows him to complete his writing assignments by
speaking into a computer. His interest in writing has increased dramati-
cally, and many of his typically developing peers have started using the
software themselves to improve their fluency and increase their writing
productivity.

Enhanced Human Resources

"Enhanced human resources" refers to the building up of a rich
network of individuals who support the growth and development of
a neurodiverse student. Such a network might include many of the
following individuals:

- Regular and special education teacher
- Psychologist or counselor
- Social worker
- Speech and language therapist
- Personal tutor or academic coach
- Physical, occupational, music, or drama therapist
- Teacher's aide
- Parents and relatives
- High school or college-aged volunteers
- Peers and younger or older students

Interventions to enhance a student's human resource network might involve

- Strengthening the student's most life-affirming relationships,
- Reinvigorating existing relationships that are faltering, and
- Fostering new relationships that will enhance the student's life.

Example of poor niche construction: Nate is a 1st grader with ADHD. He has been having problems getting along with his regular classroom teacher, who wants him placed in a special day class. His peers have been giving him a hard time about this during recess. He has increasingly been involved in fights with classmates and seems to have no close friends. A psychologist described Nate as combative, uncooperative, and angry.

Example of positive niche construction: Jose is a 1st grader with ADHD who has been having problems with his regular classroom teacher. A series of meetings are held after school to help resolve much of the conflict between them, resulting in a better relationship. In addition, a 5th grade student has become a "buddy" to Jose and plays ball with him every day at recess. Jose has started to form tentative friendships with his peers.

Strength-Based Learning Strategies

Students are placed in special education programs because, for one reason or another, conventional approaches to teaching and learning have failed to help them. These students require innovative approaches to learning that have not yet been tried with them and that build upon their particular strengths, interests, and abilities. So, for example, teaching reading fluency through song lyrics for a child with Down syndrome who loves singing and music may be an effective learning strategy for that particular student. Although many of the strategies in this book are research-based, it's important to remember that we need to use differentiated learning strategies that reflect the *unique* strengths of each student, not just strategies that appear on an approved list of "evidence-based" interventions. The idiosyncrasies, nuances, and complexities of the teaching process all point to the fact that a teacher's own experiences, beliefs, and values may frequently be more decisive for a child's learning progress than research findings (see, for example, Biesta, 2007; Clegg, 2005).

Example of poor niche construction: Sal is a 3rd grader with learning disabilities who struggles with his reading. He is taken out of regular reading class and spends an hour a day in a resource room working on a phonemic awareness program that he says is "boring." His regular classroom teacher is concerned that his time in the resource room is making him fall further behind his classmates in the regular classroom.

Example of positive niche construction: Ivan is a 3rd grader with learning disabilities who struggles with reading. He has a vivid imagination, loves drawing, and prefers working with pictures rather than words. Both his regular classroom teacher and his special education teacher have been using highly illustrated books (including pop-up books), letting him draw pictures of vocabulary words, teaching him to visualize what he's read, and giving him time each day to work with a highly graphic software program that assists him with his phonemic awareness skills.

Affirmative Career Aspirations

Children's hopes and dreams for the future often serve as stepping-stones to a stronger sense of purpose and direction in life. For many neurodiverse students, however, dreams of the future may be obscured by a sense of futility, limited expectations, and learned helplessness. In such cases, it is important for teachers to nurture the students' aspirations. At the middle and high school levels, it may be especially important for teachers to suggest future careers that students might be well suited for, given their unique constellation of abilities. So, for example, students with learning disabilities who possess high visual-spatial abilities might be encouraged to consider a future in art, graphic design, architecture, filmmaking, or engineering. Students with ADHD could be asked to think about careers that involve novelty, movement, or change, such as firefighting, newspaper reporting, surveying, or fitness instruction. High-functioning students on the autistic spectrum may be encouraged to consider vocations that involve systems, such as mathematics, computer programming, science, mechanical repair, or accounting. A student with intellectual disabilities might be encouraged to aspire to postsecondary education or perhaps to a future as a childcare worker, a veterinary assistant, or a hospital attendant. In each of these cases, encouraging students to aspire to careers that suit their strengths can provide them with a sense of meaning and purpose in life.

Example of poor niche construction: Ricardo is a 12th grade student with high-functioning autism. He excels at computer programming but doesn't believe anyone will want to hire him with his disability. He has no plans for what he'll do after graduating from high school.

Example of positive niche construction: Lucille is an 11th grade student with high-functioning autism. She excels at computer programming and is told about a software firm in Denmark that hires 75 percent of its workers from the autistic spectrum because of their gifts for finding "bugs" in software. This information excites Lucille, who starts to investigate postsecondary programs that train people to become computer programmers.

Environmental Modifications

A key principle of the Individuals with Disabilities Education Improvement Act (2004) is that students in special education should be placed in the "least restrictive environment." This usually means that students need to be educated as much as possible alongside their nondisabled peers in a regular classroom. But the word *environment* has a range of other possible interpretations that may be equally important for meeting the needs of students in special education. For example, research suggests that children labeled ADHD perform particularly well in "green" (i.e., natural) environments (Kuo & Taylor, 2004). For such students, the outdoors may prove to be the "least restrictive environment." Similarly, students on the autistic spectrum who have hypersensitivity to sounds may perform better in an environment where school bells are muffled and chairs are padded to avoid squeaking. Those with emotional or behavioral issues may benefit from having a space to go to in the school where they can "chill out" after a meltdown. Finding or creating environments where students' cognitive, emotional, social, or physical strengths have the best chance of being reinforced is what matters most here. This means viewing the whole school and even the surrounding community as a complex network of possible microhabitats for meeting the varied needs of students with special needs.

Example of poor niche construction: Julie is a high school junior with an emotional disorder and learning disabilities. She struggles with coursework and is bored in both her regular and special education classrooms. Her teacher thinks she may also have ADHD because of her difficulty concentrating in class. Julie has been referred to the special education teacher for more testing.

Example of positive niche construction: Jason is a high school senior with an emotional disorder and learning disabilities. He struggles with coursework and is bored in class. He really enjoys working with his hands and especially loves building furniture in his spare time. His school counselor learns of this and arranges for Jason to spend his afternoons involved in an apprenticeship program in furnituremaking at a local community college.

Common Core Standards Assessment for Students with Special Needs

The establishment of appropriate assessments for students with special needs based on Common Core Standards must represent a flexible process where the students' own abilities and challenges are taken into consideration. Guidelines issued by the authors of the Common Core State Standards Initiative indicate that for students with disabilities to achieve at high levels on these national standards, appropriate accommodations need to be put into place. According to the authors, these accommodations should include: changes in materials or procedures, an Individualized Educational Program (IEP), specialized instructional support personnel, assistive technologies, and instructional supports for learning (including Universal Design for Learning). The authors indicate that UDL in particular encompasses a range of strategies "which foster student engagement by presenting information in multiple ways and allowing for diverse avenues of action and expression" (Common Core State Standards Initiative, 2011). Thus, the Common Core Standards Initiative aligns directly with four components of positive niche construction described in this book: assistive technologies and Universal Design for Learning, enhanced human resources, strength-based learning strategies, and environmental modifications. In addition, the other three components of positive niche construction—strengths awareness, positive role models, and affirmative career aspirations—can be characterized as additional supports for students with special needs in meeting the requirements of the Common Core Standards.

The Center for Applied Special Technology (CAST) has observed that some Common Core Standards may present substantial obstacles to students with disabilities. Take the following example: *1.MD.3—Tell and write time in hours and half-hours using analog and digital clocks.* CAST suggests that this standard (and others like it) may prove to be an insurmountable barrier for students who have difficulty writing. They suggest that the word *express* be substituted for *write* so that students with disabilities have other ways of reaching the objective. Alternatively, they suggest that the word *write* be interpreted broadly to include other means of expression (Center for Applied Special Technology, 2012). This flexible approach to assessment based on strengths should be followed throughout the Common Core Standards. In this way, students with special needs can be challenged to reach high levels of performance using their unique patterns of learning and behaving.

Conclusion

The concept of neurodiversity suggests that we shift paradigms from one based on deficits and "remediation" (literally, the reconnecting of what has been damaged) to one based on the cultivation of strengths. Just as animals in the wild work methodically to build an environment that best suits them, educators should work diligently to construct a positive niche that fits the unique needs of each individual child with special needs. We will explore the use of positive niche construction for several disability categories in the following chapters.

For Further Study

1. **Examine the quality of the discourse among teachers at your school regarding students with special needs.** Do the statements that teachers make about students reflect more of a deficit orientation (e.g., "You know, he's really low in math and has terrible reading comprehension skills") or more of a strengths-orientation (e.g., "He's got this great attitude and yesterday drew the most amazing doodle on his math worksheet")? See if you can count, over the course of a day, the number of positive and negative statements that you hear about students with special needs at your school. What does this experience teach you about your or your teachers' implicit attitudes about these students?

(Continued on next page)

For Further Study *(Continued)*

2. **Read some of the literature in the emerging field of neurodiversity.** Possibilities include Thomas Armstrong's *The Power of Neurodiversity,* Sarah Hendrickx's *The Adolescent and Adult Neuro-diversity Handbook,* Susanne Antonetta's *A Mind Apart,* and the *Disability Studies Quarterly* special issue, "Autism and the Concept of Neurodiversity." Alternatively, read one or more books by neurologist and essayist Oliver Sacks. My personal favorites are *An Anthropologist on Mars* and *The Man Who Mistook His Wife for a Hat.* How does your reading help to shape your feelings and thoughts about the need to see students with special needs in a new and more positive way?

3. **Reflect on how Response to Intervention (RtI) and Positive Behavioral Interventions and Support (PBIS) align with the concepts of neurodiversity and positive niche construction as described in this chapter.** Write about or discuss with colleagues how these concepts might be integrated within an RtI or PBIS framework.

4. **Use the seven components of positive niche construction discussed in this chapter to evaluate the experiences of one or more students with disabilities at your school.** Would you characterize these students as being in positive or poor niches? If the students are in poor niches, describe the practical steps that need to be taken to construct more positive niches for them.

5. **Select one of the components of positive niche construction discussed in this chapter and find out more about it through reading, classroom observations, or action research.** Plan a project, paper, or presentation focusing on the potentially positive impact of this component on one or more of the students with special needs in your school.

6. **What are the implications of neurodiversity for how we structure special education in the United States?** How might special education be different if politicians, administrators, and teachers took neurodiversity more seriously? Write a position paper or conduct a discussion group that focuses on these questions.

2 | The Multiple Talents of Students with Learning Disabilities

I was considered slow. While my classmates were reading their textbooks, I drew in the margins.

—*Robert Rauschenberg, artist*

I was blessed with many remarkable students who had learning disabilities in my special education classes over the years. One of them, a 13-year-old boy, held the national record in his age group for the breaststroke in swimming. Another, a girl of 9, was a model for a national department store chain. A third, a 10-year-old girl, was being investigated by parapsychologists because she purportedly could send an "imaginary playmate" into a room with no one in it and "read" the page numbers out of an open dictionary. Many others were storytellers, artists, cartoonists, and mechanical geniuses. I was always puzzled by the fact that teachers in the school didn't see the positive side of these kids. Of course, I knew that it was because these students had failed in the most important subjects that the school valued: reading, writing, and math. Part of my task was to help them master these skills. But another aspect of my work was to help them recognize their strengths as well as their difficulties.

Learning disabilities are the most common reason that children are referred for special education services in the United States, representing about 5 percent of all students in public schools (U.S. Department of Education, 2011). The more precise term *specific learning disabilities* refers to a broad range of disorders that affect reading, writing, listening, speaking, reasoning, calculating, sensory processing, and memory. Students can have one or more of these disorders at the same time. Of all students with specific learning disabilities, up to 80 percent have deficits in reading. Although there are many different types of reading disabilities, the most common form is developmental dyslexia. We will be focusing primarily on this disorder in the course of this chapter.

People used to think that people with dyslexia had trouble with the visual aspects of words. In fact, many still believe that one key symptom of dyslexia is letter reversal (giving rise to the famous joke: "dyslexics of the world, *untie!*"). However, recent research suggests that dyslexia is, at least in large part, a phonological disorder. Individuals with dyslexia have trouble discriminating many of the 45 phonemes in the English language (Shaywitz & Shaywitz, 2009). They have difficulty telling the difference between a "buh," a "duh" and a "puh," for example, and have trouble blending phonemes together to make whole words. Neuroscience research suggests that individuals with dyslexia have a very different pattern of brain activation compared to neurotypical readers. According to Yale psychologist Sally Shaywitz (2008), readers who have dyslexia process information with greater difficulty in two particular areas of the brain, both of them located in the left hemisphere: the "word analysis" area, which is involved in recognizing phonemes and blending them together to make whole words, and the "word form" area, the neural circuits of which allow typically developing readers to move from simple word recognition to word fluency (i.e., looking at a word and instantly knowing what it is). "If you're a good reader and you can use that word-form area well, you can look at a word and you're on the express highway to reading," says Shaywitz. "But if you're a dyslexic, that route is blocked and you have to get off and take a 'country road'—it's circuitous, and it's bumpy. You can get where you're going, but it takes a lot longer." Individuals with dyslexia often use other, less efficient areas of the brain to decipher words, including an area toward the front of the left hemisphere important for spoken language, and also certain areas of the right hemisphere.

Strength Awareness

When I did my doctoral dissertation on the strengths of children diagnosed with learning disabilities, one capacity that kept coming up was artistic ability (Armstrong, 1988). Many of these kids doodled on their worksheets, drew cartoons, made interesting three-dimensional designs, and showed promise in art class. Harvard neurologist Norman Geschwind (1982) once remarked that it is common for kids with dyslexia as young as 3 to show unusual skill in drawing, doing mechanical puzzles, or building models.

Many well-known artists—among them Andy Warhol, Robert Rauschenberg, Auguste Rodin, Jackson Pollock, and Leonardo da Vinci—have been judged as having had dyslexia. In one study at a British professional art school, almost three-quarters of the foundation-level students were assessed as having some form of dyslexia. According to the psychologist who conducted the survey, Beverly Steffert, the research "so far seems to show that there does seem to be a 'trade-off' between being able to see the world in this wonderfully vivid and three-dimensional way, and an inability to cope with the written word either through reading or writing" (Appleyard, 1997). In another study, individuals with dyslexia were able to recognize impossible three-dimensional objects (such as those made famous by the artist M. C. Escher) more quickly and efficiently than neurotypical subjects. The researchers noted that "the compelling implication of this finding is that dyslexia should not be characterized only by deficit, but also by talent. Global visual-spatial processing (what we refer to as 'holistic inspection'), may underlie important real world activities such as mechanical skill, carpentry, invention, visual artistry, surgery, and interpreting x-rays or magnetic resonance images (MRI)" (Karolyi et al., 2003, p. 430). In a study of 34 inventors who possessed high levels of mechanical/spatial ability, most reported weaknesses in writing and verbal areas, and more than half described themselves as low achievers in school who had failed at least one class (Colangelo, Assouline, Kerr, Huesman, & Johnson, 1993).

Unfortunately, little of the research concerning the gifts and abilities of individuals with learning disabilities has been incorporated into the field of special education. I'm reminded of an editorial I read in *Learning Disability Quarterly* (LDQ) in the 1980s, in which the publication's editor, Mary Poplin, explained why she was resigning from her post:

> The horrifying truth is that in the four years I have been editor of LDQ, only one article has been submitted that sought to elaborate on the talents of the learning disabled. . . . Why do we not know if our students are talented in art, music, dance, athletics, mechanical repair, computer programming, or are creative in other nontraditional ways? . . . It is because, like regular educators, we care only about competence in its most traditional and bookish sense— reading, writing, spelling, science, social studies and math in basal texts and worksheets. (Poplin, 1984, p. 133)

I recently reviewed the last 10 years of *Learning Disability Quarterly* to see if things had changed for the better. Sadly, I didn't find a single article on the talents and abilities of students with learning disabilities.

Certainly it's important to identify weaknesses and develop learning approaches to remediate those difficulties. Significant work is being done in this area: for example, reading software such as Fast For-Word and remediation programs like the Lindamood-Bell Learning Processes have been able to change the brain scans of students with dyslexia to look more like those of neurotypical readers (Temple et al., 2003). This is a tremendous accomplishment, but it leaves out a crucial piece of the puzzle: positive niche construction—that is, the building of an environment modified to fit the unique strengths of the learning-disabled brain.

Positive Role Models

One of the most important ideas for students with learning disabilities to understand is that there are many individuals out there in the real world just like them who have become successful in spite of (or perhaps because of) their condition. Fortunately, many famous individuals have been open about their learning disabilities. Figure 2.1 lists some exceptional individuals of the past and present who have struggled with reading and writing during their lives.

The Yale Center for Dyslexia and Creativity also provides biographies of successful individuals with dyslexia at http://dyslexia.yale .edu/successstories.html. Teachers might want to highlight a different personality each week in their classrooms, or assign students to look up biographies and report back to the class. Teachers should also be on the lookout for accomplished individuals in their own communities who have learning disabilities. Such community leaders should be invited to visit the school and share their stories with students.

Assistive Technologies/ Universal Design for Learning

A wide range of assistive technologies and UDL methodologies exist to help students with learning disabilities acquire information, express knowledge, and increase their motivation to learn. Audiobooks, for

2.1 Notable Individuals with Learning Disabilities	
The Arts	Robert Rauschenberg, Andy Warhol, Chuck Close, Leonardo da Vinci
The Sciences	Thomas Edison, Michael Faraday, Carol Greider, Alexander Graham Bell
Business	Richard Branson, Henry Ford, Charles Schwab, Ted Turner
Entertainment	Tom Cruise, Cher, Whoopi Goldberg, Orlando Bloom
Sports	Muhammad Ali, Greg Louganis, Nolan Ryan, Bruce Jenner
Politics & the Military	Nelson Rockefeller, Woodrow Wilson, George Patton, Gavin Newsom
Writers	John Irving, Fannie Flagg, Scott Adams, Agatha Christie

example, provide learners with access to books they might otherwise find difficult to read. Word processing programs are especially helpful, as they provide a wide range of features to help readers and writers with dyslexia: font sizes can be made larger, more ornate, or more colorful to facilitate easier reading, and background colors can be varied. In addition, the word count feature helps students keep track of their progress in writing tasks, and spell and grammar checkers spot errors and provide a means of correcting them (some programs, like Microsoft Word, automatically correct many common words that are initially misspelled). Students with learning disabilities can also use tape recorders to record lectures for playback at a later date. There are even "smart pens," such as the Livescribe smartpen, which record lectures while the student takes notes on specially constructed paper. If a student wants to know exactly what his teacher was saying when he wrote down a particular note, all he has to do is press down on the note with the smartpen and that portion of the lecture will be played back.

Many other software programs and hardware options help ease the transition from oral to written language for students with learning disabilities. Speech-to-text software, for example, translates a student's oral language into printed text on the computer screen. Students whose speaking skills are strong can use such software to generate poems, reports, essays, plays, and other written work that they might otherwise find laborious to complete. One of the most popular speech-to-text software brands, Dragon Naturally Speaking, also comes as an app for smart phones and tablets. Dragon Search uses voice commands to search for information online, and Dragon Dictate allows users to dictate email, Facebook posts, tweets, and personal notes.

There are also devices that reverse this process and translate printed text into spoken language. The Kurzweil Reader, for example, developed by futurist and inventor Ray Kurzweil, scans any printed text (e.g., book pages, menus, magazines) and reads it out loud through a synthesized voice. This allows students with learning disabilities to keep up with their peers by having a large part of their reading material read to them. Soliloquy Learning's ReadIt program allows users to read text on the screen and get help with individual words or blocks of text by clicking on the highlighted material and having the computer read the material back. The software also monitors the user's reading rate, provides definitions of words, and keeps track of words that are particularly difficult. Other devices, such as Amazon's Kindle e-reader, can be set to automatically read the onscreen text out loud. By providing both oral and written language simultaneously, closed-captioned television shows, movies, and video games provide students with both oral and written language to help them develop better reading fluency and reading comprehension.

Enhanced Human Resources

An important component of positive niche construction is the provision of a trusting relationship between a student with learning disabilities and at least one other person who can encourage that student's gifts and support her through the process of learning to read and write more effectively. This support person might be a regular classroom teacher, a special education teacher, a private reading tutor, a peer, or an older student who can serve as a study buddy. What is most important is for the role model to believe in the student and champion her cause. Discussing successful individuals with learning disabilities featured in her book *Overcoming Dyslexia,* Yale researcher Sally Shaywitz points out that "in each instance there was someone—a parent, a teacher, a coach—who truly believed in him and who helped him to develop a passionate interest in an area in which he could find success. For writer John Irving, it was his wrestling coach; for playwright Wendy Wasserstein and novelist Stephen J. Cannell, it was a college professor who saw beyond the spelling errors and slow reading to recognize and to encourage true talent" (Shaywitz, n.d.). Teachers who instruct students with learning disabilities should recognize that establishing a positive rapport with the student is sometimes as important, or even more important, than the teaching of specific reading and writing skills.

Strength-Based Learning Strategies

From the earliest days of research on learning disabilities, a multisensory strategy has been viewed as perhaps the best instructional intervention to use with students who have trouble reading and writing (see, for example, Slingerland, 1996). As students learn their letters and sounds, have them form letters in clay or with pipe cleaners, draw them on pavement with chalk, trace them in sandpaper, or manipulate them using colored blocks or tiles. Capitalizing on their strong visual-spatial skills, suggest that students write captions for photographs or draw storyboards to show their understanding of the sequence of a story. To enhance reading comprehension, tell students to close their eyes and visualize what they have just read. Some students have even found that the use of colored overlays or special lenses improve their perception of words (Williams, Kitchener, Press, Scheiman, & Steele, 2004). Reading materials should be chosen with a student's interests in mind. A student who enjoys mathematics, for example, might like to read *Counting on Frank* by Rod Clement, while a student who is fascinated with insects might enjoy Matthew Reinhart's *Young Naturalist's Handbook: Insect-lo-pedia.*

To personalize learning, show students how to take their dictated material from speech-to-text software and transform it into a book that could then be catalogued in the school library. If students exhibit music as a special strength, have them use percussion instruments to tap out the syllables of words or use singing or chanting to turn phonemes into musical sounds. This is especially helpful in addressing the phonological difficulties that many individuals with learning disabilities face (Overy, 2003).

Here are some additional strength-based strategies to use with students who have learning disabilities:

- Use video to teach specific content.
- Provide students with a camera or camcorder to record their experiences.
- Draw pictures or use graphic organizers to illustrate concepts or content (see the Education Oasis website at www .educationoasis.com/curriculum/graphic_organizers.htm for a selection of 58 possible graphic organizers).
- Use reading material that includes rich visual representations—photos, flowcharts, decision trees, diagrams, and so on.
- Teach creative thinking techniques to your students (see Michalko, 2006).

- Teach mind-mapping strategies for taking notes (see Buzan, 1996) or use mind-mapping software (e.g., Kidspiration).
- Provide software that makes use of visual-spatial skills, such as animation or graphic arts programs.
- Allow students to doodle while they're listening to lectures (see Andrade, 2010).
- Use Google's "image search" feature to find pictures that illustrate vocabulary words and concepts.
- Let students color-code texts using highlighter pens.
- Have students create imaginative pictures of their vocabulary words (see Mallet, 2011).
- Provide students with "the big picture" before going into details when teaching a subject.
- Integrate the arts into academic subjects.
- Use LEGOs, D-stix, hexaflexagons, blocks, pipe cleaners, or other three-dimensional materials to illustrate language arts concepts.

Affirmative Career Aspirations

Individuals with learning disabilities possess skills that are becoming increasingly important with the advent of new technologies in science, technology, and engineering. As author Thomas West—who himself has dyslexia—wrote in 1991:

> With further technological development, we may see striking new opportunities for these creative, visual-thinking persons. We may soon see them crossing over from the arts, their traditional stronghold, to the scientific and technical fields that have long been largely closed to them. . . . Perhaps in the future we might see the solution of difficult problems in statistics, molecular biology, materials development, or higher mathematics coming from people

who are graphic artists, sculptors, craftsmen, filmmakers, or designers of animated computer graphics. Different kinds of problems and different kinds of tools may require different talents and favor different kinds of brains. (West, 1991, p. 8)

West's predictions were right on target. In 2009, the Nobel Prize in Physiology/Medicine was awarded to the molecular biologist Carol Greider, who has dyslexia, for her work on the role of telomerase, an enzyme that protects telomeres (the ends of chromosomes) from progressive shortening. Inventor and biologist Bill Dreyer, who also has dyslexia, developed groundbreaking theories about the creation of antibodies and created one of the first protein-sequencing machines. Dreyer says that he thinks "in 3-D Technicolor images instead of words." About his protein-sequencing invention, he observed that "[I] was able to see the machine in my head and rotate valves and actually see the instrumentation. I don't think of dyslexia as a deficiency. It's like having [computer-aided design] in your brain" (Morris, 2002).

Individuals with dyslexia also show expertise in the field of business. In one study, conducted by Julie Logan, a professor of entrepreneurship at the Cass Business School in London, more than a third of self-employed business people interviewed reported having dyslexia. This compared with a national incidence of dyslexia at 10 percent of the general population and only 1 percent of corporate managers surveyed. Logan suggests that because dyslexics faced difficulty navigating their way through school, they had to develop soft skills such as problem solving, perseverance, the capacity to delegate, and excellent oral communication. Logan notes that "the ability to attack problems and solve them is essential when one is creating a new venture, so the dyslexic who has had to overcome problems to survive at school has much experience in this area" (Warren, 2008). People with dyslexia also demonstrate superior intuitive or "out-of-the-box" thinking, which can be invaluable in starting and maintaining a new business.

"Perhaps my early problems with dyslexia made me more intuitive," writes dyslexic billionaire Richard Branson. "When someone sends me a written proposal, rather than dwelling on detailed facts and figures, I find that my imagination grasps and expands on what I read" (Branson, 1998, p. 25). John Chambers, the CEO of technology giant Cisco Systems, has dyslexia and describes its effects as follows:

> I can't explain why, but I just approach problems differently.
> . . . It's very easy for me to jump conceptually from *A* to *Z*.
> I picture a chess game on a multiple-layer dimensional cycle
> and almost play it out in my mind. But it's not a chess game.
> It's business. I don't make moves one at a time. I can usually
> anticipate the potential outcome and where the Ys in the
> road will occur. (Morris, 2002)

The following careers might be particularly suitable choices for students with learning disabilities:

- Animator
- Engineer
- Physicist
- Artist
- Interior decorator
- Sculptor
- Entrepreneur
- Graphic artist
- Molecular biologist
- Graphic software designer
- Surveyor
- Architect
- Fashion designer
- Pilot
- Cartographer

- Inventor

- Surgeon

- Photographer

It's important to keep in mind that individuals with learning disabilities can achieve success in whatever field they put their minds to, including those that focus on their area of deficit. Many well-known writers have had learning disabilities, including Agatha Christie, John Irving, and Philip Schulz (winner of the 2008 Pulitzer Prize for Poetry).

Environmental Modifications

The least restrictive environment for a student with learning disabilities is a setting where difficulties with the printed word are minimized and strengths (e.g., art, architecture, graphic design, entrepreneurship) are maximized. A look at the school day, for example, would suggest that art class or shop class might be an oasis for the student with learning disabilities who must navigate several academic classes that feature a strong reading component. Even better would be an arts-oriented magnet school or one that puts a great deal of attention on science, technology, engineering, and mathematics (i.e., a STEM school). The MicroSociety method would also be a good fit for a student with dyslexia who has entrepreneurial gifts, inasmuch as the entire afternoon of such a program is given over to business-related projects and activities (for information on implementing such a program, see www.microsociety.org).

For many students, however, schoolwide programs such as these aren't an option. It even sometimes happens that a student's strongest courses are taken away to give more time for reading remediation (an example of poor niche construction). Other times, art and related courses aren't even available in school, having been cut back as a result of a growing emphasis on math and reading (see, for example, Robelen, 2012). In such cases, students might look to extracurricular pursuits as a way of getting involved in activities that capitalize on their strengths, including after-school programs in arts and crafts, entrepreneurship, and service learning. Finally, for middle and high school students with learning disabilities, apprenticeship programs with an artist, architect, graphic designer, illustrator, mechanical engineer, or other role model may be a strong environmental modification that would translate into career success.

Scenario #1: Robert

Robert is 8 years old and struggles with reading. Though he's in the 3rd grade, he reads at the kindergarten level and finds the process of reading out loud to be frustrating. His writing skills are also rudimentary: He can write the alphabet and a few basic sight words, but has a hard time putting anything meaningful on a sheet of paper. He draws exceptionally well for his age, however, and often creates doodles on his worksheets depicting cartoon characters and fancy sports cars. His mother reports that at home he is fascinated by machines and also loves to build with three-dimensional building blocks like Legos.

Poor Niche Construction

Robert is sent to a resource room program for two hours a day, where he spends most of his time filling out worksheets related to phonemic awareness, reading comprehension, and writing skills. Since starting the special education program, he has been involved in fights with other boys both inside the classroom and outside during recess. He sometimes refuses to work and is sent to the time-out area, where he often continues to misbehave. A behavior modification program has been instituted for him in which he receives points for finishing his worksheets. This has resulted in a slight improvement in his behavior, but he still complains about being in what he calls "the stupid classroom." He has shown only marginal improvement in his reading and writing skills.

Positive Niche Construction

Robert is placed full-time in a regular classroom that implements strength-based learning strategies. He begins to work with a highly interactive computer program that helps him discriminate between similar-sounding phonemes and assists him in blending phonemes into whole words. He likes the program because of its colorful displays, game-like structure, and instant feedback. His teacher has also designated him as the "class artist." Whenever students need help with a drawing or picture, they know they can call upon Robert as an advisor. He has started to write captions for several of his drawings, and he is just beginning a project that will involve creating a comic strip with colorful images and snappy dialogue. These activities are increasing his motivation to write. He often remains in the classroom during recess to work on his projects. He has begun to enjoy reading highly illustrated books and particularly likes those with a "pop-up" feature. During a recent unit on housing in different cultures, Robert announced that he would like to be an architect. His teacher arranged for an architect to come to the school and meet with Robert and a few other interested students to learn more about the profession.

Scenario #2: Brandon

Brandon is in 11th grade but still reads at the 4th grade level. He's fallen far behind his classmates in most of his subjects, especially those with a heavy reading load. As a result, he's given up on several of his courses and spends much of his time in class staring out the window. He does better in his geometry and chemistry classes, and he especially enjoys carrying out experiments, although he often has trouble writing up his results, which lowers his grade substantially. He's missed several school days this year and says that he may drop out of school at the end of the year and get a job as a construction worker.

Poor Niche Construction

Brandon is sent to a continuation high school where he takes classes alongside other potential dropouts and students with behavior and learning problems. He's been taken out of his geometry and chemistry classes and put in a special reading remediation program where the focus is on treating his disability through special booklets that focus on reading comprehension. He continues to skip class and is often found in a nearby park smoking with some of the other students from the continuation high school. On a couple of occasions, he has even been handcuffed by the local truant officer and brought back to the school in full sight of his peers.

Positive Niche Construction

Brandon is kept in his local high school and given the use of a Kurzweil Reader that scans his textbooks and reads them back to him. This has helped substantially in dealing with his heavy reading load. He's selected as a tutor in geometry class to help others who struggle with the subject. In chemistry, he's paired with a lab partner who has especially good writing skills and who is helping Brandon with his lab reports. He's been encouraged to get involved with the school's science fair this year and has begun a project on identifying the sugar content in different kinds of soft drinks. At the encouragement of his high school civics teacher, he's also begun to show an interest in student government and plans to run for student council next semester.

Sample Strategies for Applying Positive Niche Construction to Common Core State Standards

Sample Standard: ELA.RL.4.3—Describe in depth a character, setting, or event in a story or drama, drawing on specific details in the text (e.g., a character's words, thoughts, or actions).

Strength Awareness

- Find out which texts most interest the student (e.g., a specific play or story).
- Discover whether the student has specific strengths that may be used to express an in-depth understanding of the character, setting, or event (e.g., dramatic improvisation, storytelling, drawing).

Positive Role Models

Expose the student to positive examples of other students who can provide in-depth descriptions of a character, setting, or event in a story or drama.

Assistive Technologies/Universal Design for Learning

- Provide the student with access to text-to-speech software to help with the reading of the story or drama.
- Select text that has interactive features (such as a digital book) that will help the student to comprehend the text.

Enhanced Human Resources

Pair the student with a typically developing student who has strong language arts skills to help in locating textual details that support an in-depth treatment of character, setting, or event in a story or drama.

Strength-Based Learning Strategies

- Have the student use a yellow marker to highlight details in the printed text that pertain to his chosen character, setting, or event.
- Teach the student to use mind mapping to help organize details from the text.
- Select a text that has high visual content (e.g., a graphic novel).

- Let the student draw images representing each detail to be included in the in-depth study (e.g., a comic strip or storyboard).

Affirmative Career Aspirations

Find out what career aspirations the student has, and demonstrate how this core standard would be useful in the student's career. For example, if the student shows interest in a career in architecture, discuss the importance of having an in-depth knowledge of an architectural project and the value of paying attention to details when designing a structure.

Environmental Modifications

- Build a puppet theater, stage, or other performance venue for acting out specific details of a character, setting, or event in a story or drama.

- Create a mock television or radio broadcast center that the student can use to provide an in-depth look at a character, setting, or event in a story or drama. (The resulting show could even be called "In Depth.")

Assessing the Standard

Using a favorite story or drama that the student has personally selected, the student will describe in depth a character, setting, or event in a story or drama, drawing on specific details in the text (e.g., a character's words, thoughts, or actions). The student may express these in-depth descriptions and accompanying details through speaking, writing, role playing (e.g., dramatizing the life of a character in a story), drawing (e.g., creating a storyboard containing descriptions and details of the drama or story), use of miniature figures and buildings to tell the story or drama, or some other appropriate means of expression. The student is allowed to read the story or drama using text-to-speech software, a digital book, or the assistance of some other form of interactive technology.

Conclusion

It's important for educators to remember that learning disabilities like dyslexia aren't simply academic impairments but also distinct patterns of brain organization that bring with them strengths as well as difficulties. In an environment that requires heavy use of the printed word, students with dyslexia will always be at a disadvantage. But placed in an environment that requires the ability to see the big picture, to reason in unconventional ways, and to visualize solutions to problems, they may well be ahead of the game. Twenty-first century learning requires critical thinking, collaboration, and creativity—precisely the strengths many individuals with learning disabilities possess. By emphasizing these strengths in the classroom while at the same time providing support and encouragement in "the 3 Rs," we can maximize the potential of our students with learning disabilities and help to ensure their success in school and life.

For Further Study

1. **Create a unit based on famous individuals of the past or present who struggled with learning disabilities.** As you teach your students about these individuals, notice what types of questions they ask. How do these presentations seem to affect the ways in which students with learning disabilities think about themselves?

2. **Choose a UDL methodology that has not yet been used in your class and implement it for all your students.** Notice the impact that it has, particularly on your students with learning disabilities. How do these students seem to respond? Does the technology or methodology improve their learning experience? Does it intensify their engagement with the material?

3. **Select a book to read that concerns itself with the strengths associated with dyslexia.** Possibilities include the following: *In the Mind's Eye,* by Thomas West; *The Dyslexic Advantage*, by Fernette Eide and Brock Eide; *The Gift of Dyslexia,* by Ron Davis; and *My Dyslexia,* by Philip Schultz. Read the book with one or more of your colleagues and then discuss the issues that come up for each of you, especially with regard to how the book's insights contribute to a better understanding of your own students with dyslexia and other learning disabilities.

4. **Learn more about visual thinking and its application to the curriculum and to students with learning disabilities.** Possible resources (in addition to the books listed above) include the following: *Unicorns Are Real,* by Barbara Meister Vitale; *Upside Down Brilliance,* by Linda Kreger Silverman; and *Raising Topsy-Turvy Kids,* by Alexandra Shires Golan.

5. **Develop one or more lesson plans for both your students with learning disabilities and neurotypical students that integrate pictures and words using some of the suggestions from the "Strength-Based Learning Strategies" section of this chapter.** Which activities seem to be the most successful with your struggling students? Which are the least successful? What happens when you give the child with learning disabilities more opportunities to learn in visual-spatial ways?

6. **Identify students with learning disabilities in your classroom who have entrepreneurial skills.** Develop a multiweek project with them that involves starting a business either in the school or in the community (include typically developing students as well). At the end of the project, evaluate what went right with the experience and what went wrong. What does this project tell you about the entrepreneurial abilities of students with learning disabilities?

3 | The Joys of ADHD

Being ADD means you see things other people miss. When *you* [my italics] see a peach you see a piece of fruit, while I see the color, the texture, and the field where it grew. Being ADD, when I read a book about marine life, my mind allows me to travel with the fish and imagine life beneath the sea—or I can read a book about astronomy and dance among the stars.

—Matthew Kutz, 13-year-old student

Many years ago, I worked for an organization called the Educational Arts Association. The association's mission was to train teachers in various approaches for integrating the arts into the regular classroom. We had many young volunteers helping us out with all sorts of tasks. One boy in particular, a 10-year-old African American kid named Eddie, seemed to stand out from the rest in terms of his vitality and commitment. He'd travel with us to industrial sites around the Boston area looking for recycled supplies that we could use in building curriculum materials. He even helped us create instructional materials, tried them out himself, and assisted us in preparing them for teacher workshops. He was definitely an asset to the organization.

While I was involved with this association, I also was getting my master's degree in education from Lesley Graduate School in Cambridge. There, I was involved in a comparative study of several special education resource rooms in the Boston area. During one of my visits to a resource room, I unexpectedly ran into Eddie, who was a student in the school's special education program. In the course of my visit to this classroom, Eddie talked out of turn, was constantly out of his seat, and generally gave the young female teacher a very hard time. He was definitely a problem student in this particular environment. Significantly, Eddie displayed the *same* qualities of energy, excitement, and vitality in the special education class that he exhibited in the arts organization. It's just that in one setting he was a liability while in the other he was an asset. Or to put it another way, his participation in the arts organization was an example of positive niche construction, while his involvement in the special education program was an example of poor niche construction.

This experience woke me up to the importance of creating appropriate environments (positive niches) for students in special education. In today's educational climate, Eddie probably would be diagnosed with ADHD, given medication for his hyperactivity, and put in a behavior modification program designed to keep him in line. The prevalence of ADHD in the United States has increased dramatically in the past few years. The Centers for Disease Control reports that ADHD diagnoses increased by a whopping 21.8 percent from 2003 to 2007—from 7.8 percent to nearly 10 percent of all schoolchildren (Centers for Disease Control and Prevention, 2010). Symptoms of ADHD include hyperactivity, distractibility or inattention, and impulsivity. It's generally believed that ADHD is largely a genetic condition that affects the brain in several regions including the frontal lobes, the limbic system, and the reticular activating system. Faulty dopamine receptors seem to impair the frontal lobes' ability to inhibit motor activity and emotional reactivity in the limbic system and also negatively affect the executive functions of the frontal lobes, which regulate problem solving, planning, and reasoning. The primary treatments or interventions for ADHD are psychoactive medications such as Ritalin or Strattera, behavior modification programs, and classroom accommodations such as assisting the students in the completion of short-term goals and working with them on basic organizational skills.

Many of the strategies recommended in books on ADHD are aimed at shoring up weaknesses in the student. However, there are a wide range of strategies based on strengths and abilities that can be part of a comprehensive program of positive niche construction.

Strength Awareness

In looking at the strengths of students labeled as ADHD, it may be useful to first consider why the genes for ADHD are still in the gene pool. There is some evidence that ADHD traits actually fulfilled an important function in prehistoric times: An individual out in the wild needed to have relatively quick motor activity (hyperactivity) in order to forage for food, find shelter quickly, and attend to other important tasks. He also needed to rapidly shift his attention from one stimulus to another (distractibility), so that he could scan the environment for signs of predators and other potential threats. Finally, he had to be able to respond quickly to his instincts (impulsivity) in order to meet whatever threats he encountered from animals, humans, weather, or other dangers (Jensen et al., 1997). It's entirely possible that people who had these ADHD genes were more likely to survive and pass their genes on to subsequent generations. One contemporary writer, Thom Hartmann, has suggested that kids with ADHD are actually hunters in a farmer's world (Hartmann, 1997). In many ways, the conventional classroom caters to the "farmers" of the world. The behaviors necessary for being a successful farmer—staying in one place, being patient, and focusing on the job at hand—are also associated with successful learning in a traditional classroom setting. The task for educators, then, is to figure out how to create environments for children with

ADHD that make use of the talents of the "hunter" without turning the classroom into a jungle!

One of the most interesting things about ADHD is that its three primary symptoms can be described either positively or negatively. A few years back, Bonnie Cramond, a professor of creative studies at the University of Georgia, noticed that the symptoms of ADHD matched up closely with the traits commonly associated with creative people (Cramond, 1994, 1995). The only difference is that the words often used to describe ADHD characteristics—*hyperactivity, distractibility,* and *impulsivity*—are negative, while the terms used to describe creative people—*vitality, divergency,* and *spontaneity*—are positive. So it may be that we're taking creative individuals and labeling them in terms of negative attributes, when we should instead be regarding them in terms of their positive qualities. A recent study backs up Cramond's analysis. When researchers at the University of Michigan gave college students, half of whom were labeled as ADHD, a series of tests measuring creativity across 10 domains, the ADHD group scored higher on all measures, including brainstorming and generating new ideas (White & Shaw, 2011).

Whether a trait will express itself in a positive or negative way may have a lot to do with the quality of the environment in which a student happens to be situated. This certainly was the case with Eddie, who was full of divergency, vitality, and spontaneity in the arts organization but distractible, hyperactive, and impulsive in the special education classroom. We would do well, then, to consider the context before labeling a child as having ADHD. Similarly, if a child exhibits disruptive behaviors, we may want to assess his creativity (e.g., by using the Torrance Tests of Creative Thinking available from Scholastic Testing Service Inc.) to see if creativity rather than ADHD is the underlying factor.

It's also important to take into account research from developmental psychology when considering the strengths of students with

ADHD. As it turns out, the brains of kids diagnosed with ADHD develop normally, but they mature on average *three years later* than the brains of typically developing children (Shaw et al., 2007). This makes sense. We've all observed children with ADHD who act younger than their age. I can still remember one 12-year-old in my junior high school special education classroom. If he saw something that interested him on the wall, he would simply get up from his chair and walk toward it, just like a toddler. We could slap a negative term onto this phenomenon and call it *immaturity*. But there is another, more positive, way of framing this developmental lag: *neoteny*. This term refers to the retention of youthful characteristics into adult development. Scientists have suggested that neoteny is a positive development in human evolution (Gould, 1977; Montagu, 1988).

If we look at the creative geniuses of Western culture—people like Einstein, Mozart, and Picasso—we often see very childlike qualities in them. Einstein, for example, was once quoted as saying that he "never grew up"—he enjoyed exploring time and space like a child (Clark, 2001). If students labeled ADHD in fact possess these child-like—or neotenous—characteristics, then they may actually be part of a vanguard of human beings who are bringing more of their childlike characteristics—imagination, playfulness, spontaneity, vitality, creativity, and wonder—into later development. This was certainly true of Eddie, who was brimming with neotenous traits such as vitality and playfulness. We should be honoring and celebrating these tendencies and constructing positive niches where they can prosper rather than pathologizing them and seeking to restrict them in the classroom.

Positive Role Models

If we look beyond the classroom and out into the world with its many and varied niches, we see that there are actually a lot of successful people with ADHD. Figure 3.1 lists some of the most prominent examples (including a few historical figures whose biographical details strongly suggest the presence of ADHD). These examples send a

3.1	Notable Individuals with ADHD
The Arts	Leonardo da Vinci, Walt Disney, Salvador Dali, Ansel Adams
The Sciences	Thomas Edison, Alexander Graham Bell, Albert Einstein, Michael Faraday
Business	Richard Branson, Paul Orfalea (founder of Kinko's), David Neeleman (founder of JetBlue Airways), Henry Ford
Entertainment	Justin Timberlake, Jim Carrey, Robin Williams, Stephen Spielberg
Sports	Michael Phelps, Terry Bradshaw, Pete Rose, Michael Jordan
Politics & The Military	James Carville, Winston Churchill, Napoleon, John F. Kennedy
Writers	Tennessee Williams, Mark Twain, Henry David Thoreau, Emily Dickinson

positive message to kids with ADHD: "If they can make it, so can I!" Students with ADHD might want to pick their favorite historical figure and keep a photo of him or her at their desks as a reminder of how they, too, can succeed if they work hard.

Assistive Technologies/ Universal Design for Learning

Many of the tools mentioned in the previous chapter will also work well for students with ADHD. However, many additional technologies and strategies more specifically target the needs of such learners, including a wide range of educational software that teaches academic content in ways that mesh with the learning tempo of students with

ADHD. Because kids diagnosed with ADHD require a higher level of stimulation than do typically developing students, any software or app that they use should be exciting, be animated if possible, give students choices, and provide immediate feedback (Bennett, Zentall, French, & Giorgetti-Borucki, 2006). These features will harmonize best with the ways in which the brain with ADHD is wired, regardless of the subject.

The Internet is both a help and a hindrance to students with ADHD. Hypertext actually mimics the distractibility (or divergency) of the mind with ADHD. Just as we move from link to link on the web, the mind of the child with ADHD jumps from thought to thought. If students are in control of the online navigation process, this capacity can prove fruitful. However, students with ADHD might also be prone to getting lost among all the links and distracted by the many advertisements, sidebars, and other clutter on websites that they visit. Programs such as Clutter Cloak, Readability, and Pace Car help to minimize such distractions by allowing users to highlight relevant material on websites and eliminate or mask everything else around it.

Students with ADHD can particularly benefit from software dedicated to organizational skills, time management, and task completion. The iStudiez app, for example, tracks tasks and deadlines and helps with homework planning and assignments. iHomework records grades, uses a color-coded calendar, keeps track of reading assignments, and allows the user to set alarms and reminders for assignments. The Time Timer app lets students know how much time they have left to complete an activity: as the time elapses, a red disc gets smaller and smaller, providing visual feedback. Invisible Clock is an external device that looks like a pager and is designed to send vibrations or a beep at selected intervals to keep a student on task.

Neurofeedback training represents an assistive technology with great potential to improve a student's ability to concentrate. The virtual reality system Play Attention, for example, has been used in classrooms for the past 15 years and is now also available for home use. In this program, a child plays an educational computer game while wearing a helmet or armband that picks up brain waves related to attention. As long as the child concentrates, he is in control of the game—but if his mind begins to wander, the game stops. In one study conducted at Hertfordshire University in the United Kingdom, researchers using this system discovered that students with ADHD had reduced impulsivity compared to a control group of children with ADHD who did not use the system (Nauert, 2010). In another well-controlled study, children who engaged in neurofeedback training were compared with a control group of kids who played computer games intended to train attention but that didn't use neurofeedback. Both parents and teachers reported a significantly greater reduction in inattentiveness, hyperactivity, and impulsivity among the children in the neurofeedback group when compared with those in the control group (Gevensleben et al., 2009).

Enhanced Human Resources

Creating a rich network of human relationships is vital for students diagnosed with ADHD, many of whom have social difficulties and need as much interpersonal support as possible. A student's regular or special education teacher can serve as an academic "coach" to help him throughout the school day. If the student fails a test or misses an assignment, the teacher might ask, "What might you have done differently?" Teachers as coaches can help students with ADHD set goals, stay motivated, and reflect on work that they've completed. Rather than functioning as a "parrot teacher" constantly reminding the student to pay attention or remember homework, the teacher coach sits down with the student and helps generate practical strategies for managing time effectively, developing study skills, and engaging in problem-solving behaviors.

Another important human resource for students labeled ADHD is peer tutoring. A peer tutor helps a student with ADHD stay on task, provides immediate feedback on the student's learning, and offers other forms of assistance as necessary. It's also a good idea for the student with ADHD to serve as a tutor at least part of the time, since this role requires mastering the skills to be learned and engages the student in taking on the added responsibility of helping another child. Studies of peer tutoring with children diagnosed as having ADHD demonstrate that this practice leads to a decrease in fidgeting, an increase in academic learning, and improved parent and teacher satisfaction when compared with control groups (DuPaul, Erven, Hook, & McGoey, 1998).

Strength-Based Learning Strategies

In a learning environment that requires students to maintain attention for a long period of time—listening to lectures, reading textbooks, completing assignments—students with ADHD will be at a distinct disadvantage compared to their neurotypical peers. Behavior modification programs that offer rewards often need to be used as incentives in such cases. These programs, however, may actually undermine a student's intrinsic motivation and love of learning (Armstrong, 1997; Kohn, 1999). In addition, externally controlling behavior modification programs tend to maximize the weaknesses of the student (by demanding that a person with a short attention span pay attention for a long period of time) and minimize the strengths. As we've observed, students with ADHD often have strengths such as vitality, divergency, spontaneity, playfulness, imagination, and curiosity. Teachers need to make use of learning strategies that address these strengths. Whenever possible, learning strategies for students with ADHD should

- Be delivered in short, dynamic segments.
- Have high emotional content.
- Deal with some aspect of creativity.
- Activate the child's imagination.
- Employ humor.
- Provide immediate feedback.

- Relate to their personal life.

- Utilize novel situations.

- Involve frequent "state changes" (e.g., sitting, then standing, then group work, then individual work).

If a student is in 2nd grade reading, for example, avoid long stretches of silent reading and boring textbooks. Instead, select reading material with emotional content (e.g., Judith Viorst's *Alexander and the Terrible, Horrible No Good Very Bad Day*) and break up the time period into shorter segments (e.g., students might spend 10 minutes reading silently, then read with a peer, then imagine their own "horrible no good very bad day," and finally draw a picture of such a day or act it out for the class).

Here are some other strength-based learning strategies for working with kids with ADHD:

- Select learning activities that involve physical movement (e.g., standing up on vowels and sitting down on consonants to learn spelling words).

- Provide hands-on learning activities (e.g., making a three-dimensional relief map to learn about geography).

- Use color to highlight learning content (e.g., emphasizing vowel digraphs by coloring them red).

- Teach self-talk skills (e.g., "If I get stuck on a test question, I'll come back to it later").

- Teach physical relaxation skills to focus and discharge energy (e.g., yoga, progressive relaxation, deep breathing).

- Use guided imagery to teach lessons (e.g., take students on an imaginary journey through the digestive system in science class).

- Give instructions in attention-grabbing ways (e.g., pantomime a four-step procedure for long division).

- Play appropriate background music through individual earphones while the students study.
- Provide students with choices (e.g., a range of possible reading materials).
- Establish consistent rules, routines, and transitions.
- Offer students real-life tasks to complete (e.g., watering the plants, serving as playground monitors, maintaining art supplies).

Affirmative Career Aspirations

A few years ago, I was on a plane headed to Europe and happened to sit next to a man of about 30 who told me he'd just been diagnosed with ADHD. I asked him what he did for a living. He said that he made religious documentaries in different parts of the world. He enjoyed his work, and for good reason—his ADHD was matched to his career. He'd go to a foreign country and work on a project for a few weeks; then, just about when he might start to get bored, the project would end and he would move on to another project in another part of the globe. This man's experience alerted me to the fact that there are many fulfilling career options out there for individuals diagnosed with ADHD. The jobs that best suit people with ADHD are those that encourage workers to do one or more of the following:

- Be actively engaged with new situations on a daily basis
- Handle emergencies
- Be physically involved
- Do many different things in a short period of time
- Engage in creative pursuits
- Work on their own

Two good examples of ADHD-compatible jobs are firefighter and emergency medical technician (EMT). As one fire chief has noted, "the intense fast-paced world of the fire service is practically tailor-made for someone who craves, for example, constant change and adrenaline-producing situations. In turn, people with ADHD often naturally exhibit the personality characteristics—such as creativity, risk-taking, and quick decision-making—that are required of the best firefighters and EMTs" (Cohen & Bailer, 1999). Other ADHD-compatible jobs might include the following:

- Recreational worker
- Forest ranger
- Nature photographer
- Craftsperson
- Entrepreneur
- Private detective
- Itinerant teacher
- Traveling salesperson
- Truck, bus, or taxicab driver
- Journalist
- Building contractor
- Emergency-room physician
- Athlete or coach
- Airline pilot
- Surveyor

It almost goes without saying that the *worst* jobs for people with ADHD would be 9-to-5 desk jobs in large, impersonal corporations (poor niche construction). Sitting in one place for a long period of time aggravates ADHD symptoms, and an impersonal workplace limits the ability of those with ADHD to express their unique gifts. And yet, because students with ADHD are so often not aware of compatible career options, too many of them grow up only to burn out in dead-end careers—and ADHD is too often identified as the reason for the burnout.

Educators should offer students with ADHD opportunities to find out more about high-energy, high-activity occupations that make the most of their assets. Opportunities to learn about suitable vocations might include career night, field trips to places of business, individualized career counseling, and direct work-related experiences such as internships, apprenticeships, and job shadowing.

Environmental Modifications

Educators need to give a great deal of attention to the kinds of settings in which students with ADHD learn. There's evidence, for example, that when students with ADHD are placed in a "green" environment—that is, outdoors, where they can play and move around—their symptoms become less pronounced; and the wilder the environment (a forest, say, as opposed to a park), the more their symptoms are alleviated (Kuo & Taylor, 2004). In the words of Russell Barkley, a key researcher in the ADHD field, the conventional classroom is, by contrast, "their Waterloo" (quoted in Moses, 1990, p. 34).

On a visit to Norway not long ago, I discovered that most Norwegian elementary schools have what they call a *gapahuk*, an open-air structure at some distance from the school, where students engage in daily outdoor activities related to the curriculum. Admittedly, it is simply not possible for most students to spend a majority of their time in a "green" environment. However, there are many ways to integrate a "green" experience into a traditional classroom setting. Here are some examples:

- Hold science classes outdoors, where students might study weather patterns, pollution, bird behaviors, insect habitats, and other natural phenomena.
- Take field trips to outdoor places (e.g., zoos, parks).

- Provide a strong physical education program that is held outdoors as much as possible.

- Tell students to run around the school building a few times before class.

- Encourage students to walk or bike to school whenever possible.

- Engage students in a schoolwide gardening project.

- Make sure that students with ADHD spend recess out in the playground (and not indoors making up missed homework or school assignments).

In addition, educators should think about providing opportunities for physical activity indoors. One teacher explained to me that when she gets a student with ADHD in her class, she gives him two desks on opposite sides of the room. That way, if the student needs to get up and move around, he can always head toward his other desk. Another teacher noticed that the day she asked a student with ADHD to water the plants at the back of the classroom while she taught the phonics lesson happened to be the only day he got an *A* on the test. Consequently, she began giving him more errands to do around the classroom while she taught. A third teacher wrote about having a parent volunteer come into the classroom and create a lectern/desk for a student with ADHD so he could work either standing up or sitting down. The lectern also had a treadle from an old sewing machine installed so he could keep his feet in motion. Other teachers have found success in using large rubber ball chairs instead of straight-backed chairs in the classroom. Research suggests that these chairs decrease hyperactivity and increase attention in students with ADHD (Schilling, Washington, Billingsley, & Deitz, 2003).

Here are more strategies for providing students with opportunities for movement in the classroom:

- Place a "reading rocking chair" in a corner of the classroom.
- Keep a mini-trampoline in a walled-off corner of the classroom.
- Give students squeeze balls to release tension.
- Let students act out vocabulary words.
- Have students role-play or perform mini-dramas of literary or historical scenes.
- Integrate skill-related games that involve movement (e.g., Simon Says) into the school day.
- Introduce "movement breaks" during which students do calisthenics for one or two minutes.
- Allow students to quietly stand at the back of the room when they need to move.
- Create simulations in the classroom (e.g., turn the class space into a "rain forest" or "medieval castle").

Research suggests that students with ADHD are actually *under-stimulated* and require more invigorating experiences than the average student (Zentall, 2005). Ensure that students with ADHD are stimulated using some of the strategies listed above as well as project-based learning, expeditionary learning, and other active learning approaches. These approaches will help them generate less hyperactivity, impulsivity, and distractibility and more vitality, spontaneity, and divergency.

Scenario #1: Aaron

Aaron is 9 years old and has just been diagnosed with ADHD. He fidgets a great deal in class, gets out of his seat without permission, and often blurts out answers (usually the wrong answers) to questions the teacher asks. He has difficulty organizing his thoughts in writing (although his writing fluency in general is adequate), and often he has to have instructions repeated to him three or four times before he can carry them out. He frequently forgets to do his homework, usually making the excuse that he forgot to bring his books home with him. He has few friends and sometimes gets into fights with students during recess. He complains about being bullied on the playground, and yet he has been observed bullying younger children.

Poor Niche Construction

Aaron is sent to a special classroom for students with behavior disorders for most of the school day. There are 10 other boys in the classroom. Here, he picks up techniques from the other boys for manipulating teachers and insulting other students. A behavior modification program has been set up to award points to students for good behavior that can then be traded at the end of each week for special privileges and little toys. Aaron has become adept at earning points while at the same time getting away with misbehaviors when the teacher is not looking. Because he frequently forgets to do his homework at home, he usually has to stay indoors during recess to complete his assignments.

Positive Niche Construction

Aaron is kept in the regular classroom and has been given a rubber ball chair to sit on and a squeeze ball to use, which have decreased his fidgeting significantly. He loves music, so his teacher tape-records some of his favorite music along with his homework instructions, and Aaron listens to the music and instructions on a cassette player as soon as he gets home. He now rarely forgets to do his homework. His regular classroom teacher makes a point of scheduling tests and other high-focus activities right after Aaron has come in from recess or PE. As a result, his attention has improved considerably on tests and other paper-and-pencil assignments. Because Aaron loves to draw, his teacher has suggested to him that, instead of blurting out the answers to the questions she asks, he create quick drawings of the answers to show the class. This way, Aaron receives the attention he craves without interrupting the class.

Scenario #2: Lisbeth

Lisbeth is a 12th grade student who has been referred for testing because of her lack of organizational skills and frequent absences from school. Her guidance counselor has indicated that she may have ADHD. She infrequently hands in homework assignments and often gets instructions confused during tests and writing assignments. Her poor performance in school—she gets *D*s in most subjects—has placed her on a list of students at risk for failing to graduate.

Poor Niche Construction

Lisbeth is sent to detention to make up for work that she failed to do in class. Because she hates detention, she begins to miss even more days at school, claiming that she's sick when she really isn't. The school demands a doctor's note for her absences, which she forges. She's caught doing this, which lands her in even more trouble with school administrators. She's sent for testing and found to have ADD (without hyperactivity). Her IEP includes the provision that homework instructions be written down for her and that she receive instruction in study skills. Neither of these objectives results in much improvement. Lisbeth continues to daydream in class and skip school when she feels like it.

Positive Niche Construction

An assessment of Lisbeth's strengths reveals that she enjoys and has an aptitude for fashion design, possesses good social skills, and does well in art class and home economics. At her guidance counselor's recommendation, she begins to attend a community college program in the afternoons and evenings in fashion design and apparel technology, and she spends the morning at a school computer lab engaged in interactive learning units designed to help her get her GED. In the spring of her senior year, she puts on a school fashion show in the high school auditorium where models show off clothing she has designed. A local newspaper covers the event, and Lisbeth begins to put together a portfolio of her best designs with the intention of eventually becoming a fashion designer.

Sample Strategies for Applying Positive Niche Construction to Common Core State Standards

Sample Standard: *7.G.3—Describe the two-dimensional figures that result from slicing three-dimensional figures, as in plane sections of right rectangular prisms and right rectangular pyramids.*

Strength Awareness

Determine the student's strengths in hands-on learning, computer learning, learning through physical movement, or other interests and abilities to determine the most effective learning strategies for mastering this standard.

Positive Role Models

Tell the student about Albert Einstein, who probably had ADHD, and who once said, "Do not worry about your difficulties in mathematics. I can assure you that mine are still greater." Suggest that the student imagine being Einstein solving some of these geometry problems.

Assistive Technologies/Universal Design for Learning

Provide the student with access to a computer program that allows him to actually slice three-dimensional figures to derive two-dimensional planes (see, for example, the following web page from the National Library of Virtual Manipulatives: http://nlvm.usu.edu/en/nav/frames_asid_126_g_3_t_3.html?open=instructions).

Enhanced Human Resources

- Provide the student with five-minute coaching sessions, spread out over a period of time, to go over the central elements of slicing three-dimensional figures.
- Pair the student with a peer to help him stay focused when doing textbook problems based on the standard.

Strength-Based Learning Strategies

- Have the student slice volumes of clay, Styrofoam, or other concrete materials to reveal their two-dimensional planes.
- Let the student create human-sized right-rectangular prisms and pyramids out of stiff wire, and then have him physically enter each object to experience "being" a two-dimensional slice.

Affirmative Career Aspirations

Ask the student what he would like to do in adulthood, and then lead him in a guided visualization that uses the standard in his chosen field. If the student would like to be a firefighter, for example, suggest that he picture a burning house and consider the necessity of having a quick understanding of cross-sections (or "slices") of the house in order to locate the origin of the fire, find possible victims, or extinguish the fire.

Environmental Modifications

- Turn the classroom into a right rectangular prism and investigate different slices of the prism using string.
- Provide a rubber ball chair for the student to use when doing seat work involving the standard.

Assessing the Standard

The student will demonstrate his knowledge of how to derive two-dimensional figures from three-dimensional volumes by using an interactive computer program, a set of concrete manipulatives, or another "action-based" medium chosen by the student.

Conclusion

In order to help students with ADHD, it is necessary to go beyond the deficit paradigm that is too often used for students with special needs. A complete re-visioning of the student's total environment is required. Instead of providing a boring, static, one-size-fits-all classroom experience and expecting the student to fit into that environment like a round peg in a square hole, the savvy educator seeks to create a stimulating differentiated learning environment that keeps pace with the energy and shifting attention span of the student.

Twenty-first century learning requires us to process information much faster than ever before. This is actually a gift that students with ADHD possess. When this kind of forward-thinking perspective is recognized and integrated within students' IEPs, the possibilities for growth are maximized, and they can learn to transform their deficits into gifts that ultimately benefit the world around them.

For Further Study

1. **Observe one of your students with ADHD in a variety of settings (e.g., taking a test, doing a hands-on project, participating in physical education class, doing art activities, playing during recess, reading a book, participating in a small group).** In which particular contexts does he have the most difficulty? In which contexts do his strengths stand out? What lessons might you learn from your observations that could help you in constructing a positive niche for this student?

2. **Read a book that highlights the strengths of the student with ADHD.** Possibilities include *The Wildest Colts Make the Best Horses,* by John Breeding; *Right-Brained Children in a Left-Brained World,* by Jeffrey Freed and Laurie Parsons; *The Edison Gene,* by Thom Hartmann; *The Gift of ADHD,* by Laura Honos-Webb; and my own book, *The Myth of the A.D.D. Child.* Read the selected book with some of your colleagues and discuss how it applies to your students with ADHD. How does your reading of this book affect your perceptions of these students?

(Continued on next page)

For Further Study *(Continued)*

3. **Invite successful members of the community who have ADHD to come in and talk to your class about how they have learned to maximize their strengths and minimize their difficulties related to ADHD.** One good place to find volunteers may be your local chapter of Children and Adults with Attention Deficit/Hyperactivity Disorder, or CHADD. Schedule ample time for students to ask questions and share thoughts. Afterward, consider whether this experience positively affected students in your class who have been diagnosed with ADHD.

4. **Survey computer software that you have used with a student who has ADHD.** Which has been the most successful? Which has been the least successful? What can you learn from this experience about how to select computer programs in the future that will work best with these students?

5. **Set up a cross-age tutoring program in which students with ADHD tutor younger children.** Make sure that the tutors know exactly what is expected of them and have a good grasp of the content they are about to teach. After several weeks, evaluate the program's effectiveness. Did placing your students with ADHD in a more responsible role result in their showing a greater degree of maturity?

6. **Turn lesson plans you are currently using that involve seatwork or lecture into lessons that involve movement, novelty, emotion, or creativity (e.g., role playing, hands-on activities, dance, pantomime, project-based learning).** How do your students with ADHD respond to these new activities?

7. **Create a variety of environments in your classroom (e.g., round tables for group discussion, square tables for projects, open space for movement, green space with plants).** Experiment with placing your students with ADHD in each of these spaces, and notice which areas seem to work best for them. Alternatively, try out different ecological strategies with your students that take their need for movement into consideration (e.g., rubber ball chairs, squeeze balls, two desks, standing at the back of the room, relaxation strategies). Which strategies work best? Which strategies are least effective? Brainstorm with your colleagues a list of strategies that are most effective in positively channeling the energies of your students with ADHD.

4 | The Gifts of Autism

Some guy with high-functioning Asperger's developed the first stone spear; it wasn't developed by those social ones yakking around the campfire.

—*Temple Grandin, animal engineer*

One of the most fascinating people to emerge in popular culture recently is Temple Grandin. She's a best-selling author, a sought-after speaker on the lecture circuit, an award-winning professor of animal science at a state university, and the designer of one-third of the cattle machinery constructed in the United States. And she has autism. When she was 2, she still wasn't talking or relating to others, so she was taken to specialists who said that she was brain damaged. They suggested that she be put in an institution. Instead, her parents found a speech therapy nursery school for her and hired a nanny who played turn-taking games with her for hours at a time. Eventually, she began to talk and make progress socially. Her school experiences were often very difficult. As an adolescent, she would lose her temper and get into fights with classmates. She was kicked out of one school for throwing a book at a girl and was sent to a boarding school for emotionally disturbed students. Finally, a high school science teacher saw her potential and suggested that she channel her energies into science. She began to show an interest in rockets, electronics, and horses. She went on to earn a bachelor's degree in psychology and a master's degree and doctorate in animal science. She became nationally known after the broadcast of an Emmy Award–winning HBO film based on her life.

Temple Grandin's story, of course, is not typical for a person labeled as autistic. Most people with autism aren't as lucky as she was to have received such intensive support throughout her life. Most people with autism struggle each and every day with things that the rest of us take for granted: communicating basic needs, socializing with others, and understanding other people's points of view. However, Grandin's life is a testament to what can happen when caregivers and educators see *the best*, rather than the worst, in children with autism.

Currently, autism affects about 1 in every 88 children (and 1 out of 54 boys), and its numbers continue to rise (Centers for Disease Control and Prevention, 2012). The term *autism* actually refers to an entire spectrum of neurodevelopmental disorders characterized by social impairments, communication difficulties, and restricted, repetitive, and stereotyped patterns of behavior. It's said that there are as many different kinds of autism as there are people who have it—from totally nonverbal individuals with intellectual disabilities on the one hand, to superintelligent and highly verbal people with Asperger's syndrome on the other. Although the cause of autism is still unknown, one theory suggests that it results from accelerated brain growth during the first year of life that upsets the delicate system of synapses carrying nerve impulses throughout the brain. Another theory proposes that the genes in an autistic brain express themselves on a molecular level very differently from those in a normal brain. Although environmental factors seem to play some role in autism spectrum disorders (ASD), there is a high heritability factor; identical twins, for example, share autistic traits up to 90 percent of the time.

Strength Awareness

While a lot of the attention concerning autism spectrum disorders focuses on negative behaviors (e.g., hand flapping, emotional meltdowns, avoidance of eye contact), there are a number of positive attributes associated with ASD that are less well-known but that deserve to be highlighted. People on the autism spectrum tend to be particularly skilled at perceiving details as opposed to whole gestalts. Children with ASD do better than their typically developing peers, for example, on the block design test of the Wechsler Intelligence Scale for Children (WISC-IV), which requires taking blocks that are all white, all red, or mixtures of red and white and putting them together to match a preexisting pattern (Shah & Frith, 1993). They also do better than neurotypical children on the embedded figures test, which requires subjects to find simple geometric shapes embedded in more complex patterns or drawings (Baron-Cohen, 1998; Shah & Frith, 1983).

Essentially, people with ASD are "Where's Waldo?" experts: They're able to pick out seemingly irrelevant details that others miss. This ability has led some researchers to suggest that individuals with autism experience what has been termed "weak central coherence"—that is, they fail to grasp the whole of a situation and perceive mainly the constituent parts. But this is a deficit-oriented way of putting things. A more positive way of saying the same thing is that individuals with autism possess "strong local analysis"—or what some researchers refer to as *enhanced perceptual functioning* (Mottron et al., 2006). This ability helps explain why the IQ scores of children with autism are 30 to 70 percentile points higher when a highly figural IQ test like the Ravens Progressive Matrices is used to measure their intelligence rather than a test that is more verbal and interpersonal such as the widely used WISC-IV (Dawson, Soulières, Gernsbacher, Mottron, 2007; Mottron, 2011).

According to Cambridge University researcher Simon Baron-Cohen, individuals with ASD are also particularly good at what he has termed *systemizing* (Baron-Cohen, 2003). Baron-Cohen suggests that there are intrinsic gender differences between people who are "empathizers" on the one hand (mostly females), and those who are "systemizers" on the other (mostly males). Empathizers have built-in sensitivities to the moods, intentions, and thoughts of other people. These are faculties that autistic individuals have great difficulty displaying. On the other end of the spectrum, however, there are the systemizers—individuals who may not relate well to people, but who love to engage with systems such as machines, computer programs, mathematical equations, drawings, or languages. Males tend toward the systemizing end of the spectrum: They are more likely than females to enjoy talking about football games, working with machines, and spending time with computers.

Baron-Cohen suggests that individuals with autism are at the extreme male end of the systemizing continuum. This fascination with systems can be as rudimentary as a nonverbal child's obsession with a rotating fan or as sophisticated as a high-functioning teen's ability to master an abstract computer language. Baron-Cohen's theory helps to explain the existence of *savants* among autistic populations: Indeed, 10 percent of all individuals with autism are said to have savant qualities (Treffert, 2009). Savants are individuals who can, for example, rapidly calculate numbers, quickly draw complicated visual scenes, or play complex musical pieces from memory.

Given the strengths associated with ASD, there may be very good reasons why the genes for autism are still in the gene pool. In prehistoric times, it might have benefitted a tribe to have some members with an acute sensitivity to small details—who could look, for example, at two circles at a distance and tell whether they were two berries or two eyes of a predator. Similarly, it would have been advantageous for a tribe to have members who were expert systemizers, especially when it came to understanding such systems as taxonomies of healing herbs, weather patterns, or methodologies for creating shelters or inventing hunting tools.

These traits aren't limited to the prehistoric past, however: We need people who can fix machines, design computer software, repair automobiles, work on plumbing, engineer bridges, and do a thousand other systems-related tasks. Temple Grandin has said that it was her autism that allowed her to zero in on the minute perceptions that pigs and cattle pay attention to in order to create animal machinery that is humane and effective (Grandin, 2004). We need likewise to regard the special interests and gifts of our students with autism as potential doorways to school and career success.

Positive Role Models

Many individuals have achieved success despite (or perhaps because of) their ASD-related characteristics. Certainly Temple Grandin would be on that list. So would several individuals who have extraordinary savant skills. Daniel Tammet, for example, is famous for having learned Icelandic in one week and for figuring out—in his head—the value of pi to 22,000 decimal places in a five-hour period. Stephen Wiltshire, a British artist with autism, was once taken on a helicopter ride over London and upon his return drew a mural of the landscape with each and every window depicted in minute and accurate detail. Leslie Lemke, a musician with autism, played a Tchaikovsky piano concerto after having heard it only once. Each of these individuals struggles with social interactions and possesses other autistic traits, yet has unique gifts to share with the world.

Figure 4.1 lists examples of famous *nonsavant* people on the autistic spectrum. These individuals demonstrate that it's possible to have problems socializing or communicating effectively with others and still make a substantial contribution to their culture. Teachers may want to place pictures of one or more of these individuals up on the walls of their classroom and periodically point out to students with autism that they too can experience success in life.

4.1 Notable Individuals on the Autistic Spectrum	
The Arts	Glenn Gould, Erik Satie, Emily Dickinson, Andy Warhol
The Sciences	Henry Cavendish, Alan Turing, Nikola Tesla, Paul Dirac
Entertainment	Daryl Hannah, Dan Aykroyd, Marty Balin, Gary Numan
Writers	Tito Mukhopadhyay, John Elder Robison, Tim Page, Temple Grandin

Assistive Technologies/ Universal Design for Learning

Many students with autism are particularly well suited for using assistive technologies and UDL methodologies because of their preference for interacting with machines rather than people. It's telling that the emergence of the concept of neurodiversity from the autistic rights movement was actually facilitated by communication over the Internet. E-mails, chat rooms, and social media sites rely on written communication without the need for nonverbal social cues. Students with autism who find it hard to pick up on nonverbal cues thus have one less thing to worry about when they're online. Moreover, the recent technological revolution in mobile phones and tablets, with their hundreds of thousands of creative applications, has opened the door to a wide range of uses that directly serve the needs and interests of people with autism. Touchscreen interfaces allow kids to interact with content directly and effortlessly—decidedly a plus, especially for children who have difficulty manipulating a mouse or joystick or using a keyboard while looking at a screen.

There are many apps on the market that can help students with ASD communicate. The MyTalk Mobile app, for instance, allows children with autism to express their needs and desires to others through pictures, visual symbols, and audio recordings of the human voice. Stories2Learn is another app that provides a vivid way of putting together "social stories" or personalized narratives consisting of text, photos, and synthesized speech. This app can be used to help students learn routines (e.g., the procedure for handing in homework), recount experiences (e.g., a field trip to the local zoo), or learn new social skills (e.g., taking turns in a board game). The AutismXpress app helps students recognize and express basic emotions through its easy-to-use interface. Look in My Eyes is an app that rewards players for quickly focusing on the onscreen eyes of a virtual person.

Another important trend in assistive technology for autistic students is the development of robots that teach social skills. Researchers at the University of Hertfordshire in the United Kingdom, for example, have created a robot called KASPAR that has shaggy black hair, striped red socks, and a baseball cap. The robot is programmed to do things like smile, frown, laugh, wave his arms, and blink (Dautenhahn et al., 2009). In New Zealand, scientists and designers have created a furry quadruped they've named Auti that responds positively with movement during friendly interactions such as soft speaking or stroking and immediately shuts down in response to problematic behaviors such as screaming or hitting. As one researcher and developer of robots for kids with ASD explained, "Children with ASD typically feel more comfortable with robots than with other people initially because robot interactions are simpler and more predictable and the children are in control of the social interaction" (Krane, 2010).

Enhanced Human Resources

Establishing a network of positive social interactions is vitally important for students with ASD. Because social interactions do not come naturally to them, educators must consider ways to infuse regularity, safety, warmth, appreciation, playfulness, and mutuality into the hundreds of interactions that they will have over the course of a school day.

The use of behaviorism, in which external rewards are used to reinforce positive behaviors, has dominated the field of autism (see, for example, Foxx, 2008). However, a more personalized way of managing interactions with autistic students is the DIR/Floortime model developed by Stanley Greenspan and Serena Wieder (Greenspan & Wieder, 2009). Instead of using artificial incentives to mold appropriate social behaviors, this model instead starts with a child's existing social behaviors, however rudimentary, and builds on them to create playful interactions. Basic elements of the model include observation, opening circles of communication, following the child's lead, extending and expanding play, and letting the child close the circle of communication.

So, for example, if the student begins waving his hands around randomly during a lesson on the knights of the Middle Ages, the teacher might say something like, "Jimmy, you need a magic sword to slay those dragons!" and then hand him a ruler to use as a magic sword. Or, if the student starts yawning during a science lesson on the respiratory system, the teacher might say, "Wow! Pete, you're really taking a lot of air into your respiratory system!" When the child initiates a positive interaction with another child, the teacher might look for opportunities to keep the interaction going. For example, if he lends his paint brush to a classmate during an art activity, the teacher might say something like, "You're being awfully generous to Sally. I'd like to be generous too. Here are some different-colored paints for you to work with. Boy, that dog you're painting looks hungry! Should we find something good for him to eat?"

This kind of attention to playful social interaction requires patience and a good deal of one-to-one time with the student. Consequently, the use of an assistant, teacher's aide, parent volunteer, college intern, or other helper to interact with the child greatly expands the opportunities for progress. Also, the best learning activities that allow for this kind of social connection aren't those that place a primacy on lectures, worksheets, and rote learning, but rather those that rely on hands-on learning, activity centers, project-based learning, expressive arts, role play, and other active learning techniques. Peer learning is also an effective intervention for students with autism. When such students are paired in a structured learning activity with a socially competent peer, especially one who is older, research suggests that learning dividends can be great (Zhang & Wheeler, 2011).

Finally, although not exactly a "human" resource, *animals* have proven to be an effective socializing tool for kids with ASD in the classroom. Because many students on the autism spectrum relate better to pets than to people, involving them in a daily routine of animal care helps them to develop a sense of responsibility, improves their decision-making and problem-solving skills, and engages them in positive social interactions with adults and peers in school (Law & Scott, 1995).

Strength-Based Learning Strategies

Paying attention to the gifts and abilities of children on the autism spectrum, and especially to their special interests, is of paramount importance in helping them realize their full potential. Although the interests of kids with ASD have been referred to by some researchers as "obsessions," "compulsions," or "fixations," these are negative ways of characterizing what should be considered a genuinely positive phenomenon. In one study of kids with Asperger's syndrome, 90 percent were seen to have special interests in subjects as diverse as shoes, World War II propeller planes, toilet brushes, the passenger list of the *Titanic*, waist measurements, the livery of Great Western trains, Rommel's desert wars, paper bags, globes and maps, oil paintings of trains, light and darkness, industrial fans, photocopiers, yellow pencils, and deep fat fryers. The study found that the students' involvement in their special interest areas was correlated with improvements in their social, communication, emotional, sensory, and fine motor skills (Winter-Messiers, 2007).

Teachers should look for ways in which a student's special interests can be used to help teach different parts of the curriculum. A student who shows a special interest in skyscrapers, for example, could read the book *Skyscraper Going Up,* by Vicki Cobb, estimate the number of windows in the Empire State Building as a math exercise, investigate the engineering methods necessary for building a skyscraper, and research the social history of how skyscrapers actually get built. Teachers should consider making students with autism "classroom experts" in their special interest areas and provide them with opportunities during class time to share any collections, projects, or information they have acquired in the course of pursuing their interests. Teachers might also have students create a portfolio consisting of items related to their interests. Sharing interests in this way can help students gain self-esteem and promote peer acceptance.

According to Temple Grandin, many children with autism require visual as opposed to auditory ways of learning (Grandin, 1996). Consequently, verbal instructions should take a backseat to visual presentations, including the use of video to model appropriate social behaviors like turn taking and sharing. In addition, hands-on manipulatives ought to be used to teach basic concepts in math and science, and procedural instructions that use images as guides can be of great benefit (e.g., the image of a school bell to signify the beginning and end of the school day, a spoon to represent lunch, a notebook to indicate turning in schoolwork, a broom to signal clean-up time).

Students with autism should have access to visual resources that provide them with opportunities to succeed, including visual puzzles (e.g., *Where's Waldo?*), art materials, and heavily illustrated books and magazines. The ability of students with autism to identify tiny details that others miss should be highlighted whenever possible; they could be made "lost and found" experts, for instance, helping to locate missing items in the classroom. Teachers should also emphasize *details* before presenting "the big picture." For example, rather than simply telling the student that "sharing is a good way to make friends," the teacher might provide several short role plays that illustrate the concept.

Remember that individuals with autism tend to prefer working with systems rather than people—including the systems of schedules, daily routines, and transitions that make up the school day. Most kids with autism have a high need for regularity and require predictable routines that they can count on. Provide them with visual schedules, calendars, and agendas that will allow them to anticipate the sequence of events that occur on a regular basis. When teaching, use concrete materials, graphic organizers, and other systems whenever possible to illustrate concepts in the curriculum. In a lesson about the history of mathematics, for example, bring in an abacus to illustrate how other cultures did their calculations in times past, or, in a lesson about electricity, display the kind of apparatus that Ben Franklin used in his early investigations of the subject.

Finally, it's important that teachers respect the desire of their students with autism to work alone. Socialization is certainly an important part of living in a democratic society, and teachers should pay a great deal of attention to the teaching of social skills. However, if a student's proclivity is to do schoolwork on his own, he should be allowed at least some time during the school day to do this. As Baron-Cohen has pointed out, "a child with AS [Asperger's syndrome] who prefers to stay in the classroom poring over encyclopedias and rock collections during break-time, when other children are outside playing together, could simply be seen as different, not disabled" (Baron-Cohen, 2002).

Here are some other practical strategies for working with kids who have autism spectrum disorders:

- Provide a "quiet area" (such as a tented or walled-off space) where the student can periodically get away from all the stimulation of the classroom.

- Make sure the student has a clearly defined space in which to put schoolwork and personal belongings (e.g., a shelf space with clearly demarcated boundaries).

- Offer a variety of ways in which the student might express himself according to his strengths while learning something new (e.g., through pictures, movement, music).

- Model appropriate behavior using role play, video, or photos depicting social cues, appropriate responses, and self-control strategies.

- Use board games as a way to practice social interactions such as turn taking, rule following, and verbal or nonverbal communication.

- Bring in different machines or mechanical devices for the student to explore (e.g., clocks, toys, pulleys, gears).

- Use multisensory learning to teach academic skills (e.g., book-making, musical recordings, clay work), but keep in mind the autistic student's sensitivities to sensory input.

- Make sure the student has frequent opportunities for communication in the classroom (e.g., by using the "turn and talk" strategy, in which the student shares with a classmate his response to a question asked by the teacher).

Affirmative Career Aspirations

One of the first physicians to recognize autism, Hans Asperger, noted back in 1944, "We can see in the autistic person, far more clearly than with any normal child, a predestination for a particular profession from earliest youth" (quoted in Frith, 1991, p. 45). As this statement suggests, some careers are particularly suitable for people on the autistic spectrum. One software company in Denmark, Specialisterne, hires 75 percent of its workforce from the ranks of people with ASD because they find that they are especially adept at computer programming (Austin, Wareham, & Busquets, 2008). The firm tests other companies' software for bugs. It's tedious work for typically developing workers, but for higher-functioning people with autism who have computer programming skills, it plays right into their strengths (e.g., working alone, focusing on small details, engaging with systems). Specialisterne, then, is an excellent example of positive niche construction in terms of careers for highly functioning people with autism.

There are a wide range of occupations open to people on the autistic spectrum depending upon their abilities and interests. Temple Grandin (2004) recommends the following careers for those with ASD who are highly visual thinkers:

- Web page designer
- Video game designer
- Automobile mechanic
- Building or factory maintenance worker
- Photographer
- Animal trainer
- Commercial artist

For those on the spectrum who are nonvisual thinkers but are good with math, music, or fact learning, Grandin suggests the following jobs (among others):

- Accountant
- Library science specialist
- Computer programmer
- Laboratory technician
- Statistician
- Bank teller
- Piano tuner
- Clerk
- Physicist

- Taxi driver

Grandin lists the following options for individuals with autism who are either nonverbal or have poor verbal skills:

- Assembly line worker
- Building custodian
- Lawn and garden worker
- Library assistant
- Warehouse worker
- Data entry clerk

Finally, Grandin suggests that there are some jobs that would be totally unsuitable for people with autism because they involve too much multitasking or social interaction, an overwhelming sensory load, or the use of long-term memory skills. Some of the jobs that fall into this category include taxi dispatcher, airline ticket agent, air traffic controller, receptionist, casino dealer, and short-order cook. Above all, students with autism should recognize that, while they have challenges, they also have strengths that can be useful to the culture when they reach adulthood. As autism blogger Lisa Jo Rudy puts it:

> It's a common trait among autistic people: they see the parts instead of the whole. It's a problem in some settings, but a terrific attribute if you're looking for . . . deep space anomalies (as an astronomer), unique cells (as a lab technician), differences among species (as a biological researcher), particular qualities of objects (as a gemologist, antiques appraiser, or art historian). (Rudy, 2009)

Environmental Modifications

A key element in understanding the needs of students with autism is recognizing that their sensory channels are often highly sensitive and require varying degrees of modulation. Loud noises, for example, may be excruciating for some students with autism. These students may need to wear ear plugs or ear phones to block out unwanted sounds. Alternatively, the outer environment itself may need to be modified. School bells may need to be muffled with tissue or duct tape, scraping chairs may require rubber cushioning on the legs, and carpeting may need to be installed.

Similarly, kinesthetic sensations may be dysregulated in children with autism and require some form of mediation. Many students with autism dislike being touched or hugged, for example, but enjoy having gentle pressure placed on their bodies (see, for example, Temple Grandin's account of creating a special "hug machine" for herself [Grandin, 2005]). For this purpose, weighted vests are sometimes used. Because tactile sensations may be either highly pleasant or very troubling to students with autism, provide a space where they can explore tactile experiences with various media (e.g., Koosh balls, Slinkys, a box full of Styrofoam peanuts, a sandbox, modeling clay).

Many students with autism enjoy moving their bodies in space as long as they are able to control the process. Have a rocking chair available in the classroom, a swivel chair to rotate around in, or a swing or merry-go-round outdoors to soothe these students, especially in times of distress. Because visual distractions and flickering fluorescent lights may also be problematic for some children with ASD, seat them next to a window or near incandescent lighting.

Scenario #1: Pedro

Nine-year-old Pedro was diagnosed with ASD when he was 3 years old. Since that time, he has been in and out of regular education classrooms, spending some years more in a regular classroom and other years more in a special class. He works at slightly below grade level in his math class and significantly below grade level in reading. He frequently becomes anxious or agitated while doing schoolwork, especially when the material is too challenging. He'll tap his fingers on the desk nervously or rock back and forth rhythmically. Pedro doesn't like being touched and spends most of his time during recess self-stimulating ("stimming") by manipulating his fingers close to his eyes. He's highly sensitive to loud noises, which can cause him to have an emotional meltdown. Pedro loves cars and trucks, and, according to his mother, will spend hours at home making detailed drawings of them from auto magazines. He also enjoys listening to music, which seems to relax him.

Poor Niche Construction

Pedro is placed full-time in a special education resource room that also includes students with learning disabilities, behavior disorders, and speech and language difficulties. Students come in and out of the classroom all day long, and he has specialists who pull him out of class for one-to-one work at different points during the day. These disruptions to Pedro's daily routine cause him much agitation. He is also disturbed by the ringing of the school bell every 40 minutes, the squeaking of chairs in the classroom, and the frequent announcements on the school's public address system, all of which exacerbate his desk tapping and rocking. He is promised a chance to listen to his favorite music or draw cars and trucks if he behaves and does all his schoolwork, but he usually fails to do so and thus rarely has an opportunity to engage in the things he enjoys. A token economy system has been instituted to reduce the occurrence of his rocking and finger games, but it is only intermittently used and thus has had little impact on his behavior.

Positive Niche Construction

Pedro is included full-time in a regular classroom. He is given an iPad that he's used to create, with the assistance of the teacher's aide, a visual schedule of his daily routines using the Stories2Learn app. The visual schedule helps him anticipate transitions and adds a sense of predictability to his school day. Pedro also works on reading and math programs on the iPad, which have boosted his achievement level in both subjects. He's been given headphones to insulate himself from loud noises, and when he gets agitated, he's directed to go to a corner of the classroom that has a rocking chair he can use while he's working on his iPad. This intervention has almost totally eliminated his emotional meltdowns. Pedro is also working on a special project about vintage cars and trucks from the 1950s that he will present to the class. On the playground, a special area has been set up with toy cars and trucks, and Pedro has been observed there engaging in meaningful social interaction with several of his classmates.

Scenario #2: Ashley

Ashley is a 17-year-old girl with Asperger's syndrome. She keeps to herself during most of her classes, works diligently on her assignments, and receives As or Bs in all subjects except for a social science course that requires frequent interactions with peers. She especially enjoys math and science classes. She is often teased by her classmates for what is perceived as her "nerdy" behavior, and she has occasionally responded to this teasing by getting into verbal and, more rarely, physical fights with classmates between classes or after school. She's particularly interested in astronomy, which she talks about whenever she gets the chance. As a result, she is sometimes derisively called "Moon Girl" by the other students in class.

Poor Niche Construction

Ashley is pulled out of her science class to participate in a life skills course intended to make her more aware of proper social customs and to help her become better at reading social cues. She is teased by students in the regular classroom for going to what they call the "dork class." As a result of the teasing and fights, she's become depressed and angry, and her schoolwork has started to suffer. She received Cs in most of her subjects during the last semester. Her behavior has earned her a slot on the principal's list of disciplinary problems, and she is required to go to detention, where she must sit and do nothing for a 45-minute period three times a week.

Positive Niche Construction

Ashley is encouraged by the school counselor to start an astronomy club at the school, which she forms with five other students. They hold a car-wash benefit to earn enough money to buy a quality telescope, and they regularly schedule star-watching get-togethers for the school and the wider community. As a result of her involvement in the club, Ashley has gotten to know an astronomer at a local college and has started to prepare for an eventual career in that field. To help her with her college preparation, she's been allowed to create an independent study program in astronomy that integrates content in science, math, and technology and is supervised by her astronomer mentor. She likes to tell others that Albert Einstein, one of her heroes, probably had Asperger's syndrome.

Sample Strategies for Applying Positive Niche Construction to Common Core State Standards— High-Functioning Student with Autism

Sample Standard: 11–12.RST.6—Analyze the author's purpose in providing an explanation, describing a procedure, or discussing an experiment in a text, identifying important issues that remain unresolved.

Strength Awareness

Determine the student's strengths and interests in identifying the particular text(s) to use in practicing and evaluating this standard. If the student is strong in science, for example, provide texts that describe a scientific procedure or discuss an experiment.

Positive Role Models

Have the student interview scientists, historians, or technicians in the community and ask them about their purpose(s) in engaging in various aspects of their work as far as they pertain to experiments, procedures, or explanations. Have them also talk about the issues they are working on that remain unresolved.

Assistive Technologies/Universal Design for Learning

- Engage the student in computer simulation activities or experiments in science (e.g., Krucible software). Ask the student about the purpose of the activity or the experiment and whether there are any unresolved issues.

- Match the student with appropriate interactive digital nonfiction texts that include relevant questions (e.g., "What is the author's purpose?" "What is still unresolved?") and that provide immediate feedback on responses.

Enhanced Human Resources

Help the student understand the basic idea that other people have purposes that may be different from our own (a difficult concept for many people with autism to grasp). Practice role-playing "What's My Purpose?"—a game in which a teacher or peer pantomimes a purposeful action, and the student must guess the purpose.

Strength-Based Learning Strategies

- Show the student a video of a scientist describing a particular science experiment or technical procedure, and follow up with questions designed to elicit the student's understanding of the scientist's purpose(s) and still unresolved issues.

- Provide the student with graphic organizers that specify explanations, procedures, or experiments and that give prompts for the thought processes necessary to elicit an understanding of the author's purpose and still unresolved issues (e.g., "Think about why the scientist did this experiment," "Did the scientist leave some things out of her explanation that need to be explored?").

Positive Career Aspirations

Determine the student's career aspirations and ask him appropriate questions about his purpose in pursuing this career and what issues remain unresolved. Then, link this discussion to the interpretation of texts as defined in this standard.

Environmental Modifications

Allow the student ample time to work alone on curriculum materials relating to this standard at a desk, study carrel, or computer station.

Assessing the Standard

The student shall analyze an author's purpose in providing an explanation, describing a procedure, or discussing an experiment in a text, identifying important issues that remain unresolved using an appropriate text of the student's choosing. The teacher shall provide prompts and allow the student's means of expression to be embodied in a computer software program (e.g., word processor, spreadsheet, web-based application). Students may use an augmentative alternative communication device if needed.

Conclusion

There is still a great deal about autism that we don't understand. Because of their difficulties with communication skills and relating to others, most students with autism are unable to tell us what they really need in the classroom. This means that, as educators, we must "read" their behaviors as best we can. But if we only see negativity in those behaviors, we're likely to come up short in giving these students what they truly require. Instead, it's important that we see the best in these kids as much as possible. This means regarding "obsessions" as special interests, seeing "meltdowns" as cries for help in modifying the sensory and emotional environment, and characterizing "inflexibility" about routines as a proclivity for working within a structured system. This doesn't mean wearing rose-colored classes and being unrealistic about who these kids really are. Instead, it means activating the constructive energies necessary to help them feel at home in the classroom and find a secure place for themselves in life.

For Further Study

1. **Find out more about the views of Temple Grandin, whose insights have transformed the way we think about autism.** Read one of her books, such as *Animals in Translation, Thinking in Pictures, The Way I See It, Emergence: Labeled Autistic,* or *Developing Talents* (the last of which deals with career possibilities for people with autism). Watch the HBO biography of her life, *Temple Grandin* (available on DVD). What might we conclude from investigating her life and ideas about how to help students with autism become successful in school and life?

2. **Observe one or more students with ASD in a classroom setting.** What can you learn about their strengths (e.g., paying attention to details, working with systems, having special interests, thinking visually)? What sorts of projects, activities, or materials might you provide that will enable the students to use these strengths more often in the classroom? For more strategies, read one of Paula Kluth's books: *Just Give Him the Whale: 20 Ways to Use Fascinations, Areas of Expertise, and Strengths to Support Students with Autism,* or *"You're Going to Love This Kid!": Teaching Students with Autism in Inclusive Classrooms.*

3. Find out more about the DIR/Floortime approach for guiding interactions with children on the autism spectrum as developed by developmental psychologists Stanley Greenspan and Serena Wieder. Read their book, *Engaging Autism: Using the Floortime Approach to Help Children Relate, Communicate, and Think.* Investigate schools that are currently using the Floortime model (for information, go to www.icdl.com/usprograms/schools/DIRSchoolsUSInternl.shtml).

4. Explore the world of applications (for computers, tablets, or smart phones) that can be used with children on the autistic spectrum (see, for example, the iTunes app Autism Apps for a comprehensive list of apps used by people diagnosed with autism). Select one or more apps to use with your students who have autism and evaluate their effectiveness in improving behavior or supporting academic learning.

5 | The Strengths of Students with Intellectual Disabilities

Having Down syndrome is like being born normal. I am just like you and you are just like me. We are all born in different ways, that is the way I can describe it. I have a normal life.

—*Chris Burke, actor*

When Jason Kingsley was born with Down syndrome in 1974, the obstetrician told his parents that he would never be able to learn. They said that he should be sent to an institution for the rest of his life, and that they should tell their friends and relatives that he died in childbirth. Fortunately, his parents didn't listen to the doctor. Instead, they took him home and raised him with great love, care, and respect. Jason appeared in 50 episodes of *Sesame Street,* where his mother was a writer, as well as in episodes of the TV shows *The Fall Guy, All My Children,* and *Touched by an Angel.* In his 20s, he cowrote a book called *Count Us In: Growing Up with Down Syndrome* with a friend who also has Down syndrome. In the book, Jason reflects on what he wishes he could say to his obstetrician about his life now if he had the chance:

> I would say, "People with disabilities *can learn!*" Then I would tell the obstetrician how smart I am. Like learning new languages, going to other foreign nations, going to teen groups and teen parties, going to cast parties, becoming independent, being . . . a lighting board operator, an actor, the backstage crew. I would talk about history, math, English, algebra, business math, global studies. . . . I will tell him that I play the violin, that I make relationships with other people, I make oil paintings, I play the piano, I can sing, I am competing in sports, in the drama group, that I have many friends and I have a full life. (Kingsley & Levitz, 1994, p. 28)

People with intellectual disabilities—usually defined as having an IQ score of 70 or below and impairments in daily functioning such as communication, self-care, social interactions, and academic achievement—are capable of many wonderful things. They've written books, kept diaries, given speeches at national conferences, passed regents exams, gone to college, become accomplished artists, developed expertise in sports, held significant jobs, and achieved many other things besides. Although it is true that these accomplishments have been achieved by a relatively small percentage of those with intellectual disabilities, the fact remains that among the chief obstacles faced by people with intellectual disabilities are the limiting expectations that others have for them. Research reveals that portrayals in the media of people with intellectual disabilities tend to show them as one-dimensional objects of pity (Pardun, 2005). People with intellectual disabilities encounter social exclusion, stigma, prejudice, and other barriers that restrict their ability to have a full and productive life. Fewer than 11 percent of students with intellectual disabilities are fully included in regular education classrooms (Smith & O'Brien, 2007). It seems clear, then, that many students with intellectual disabilities simply haven't been given the chance to realize their gifts inside or outside school.

Strength Awareness

Because one of the main criteria used in identifying intellectual disabilities is a low IQ score, it deserves pointing out that IQ tests have come under increasing criticism from educators and psychologists in recent years (see, for example, Brooks, 2007). Complicating factors can lower an individual's IQ irrespective of actual cognitive ability. It's been argued, for example, that 77 percent of Down syndrome children have visual defects and 62 percent have hearing loss, and that these factors, along with persistent low expectations, may be depressing these kids' IQ scores (Borthwick, 1996). IQ tests also restrict the field of human potential to a narrow band of abilities. Howard Gardner (1993) has written about the drawbacks of IQ testing, noting that it focuses mainly on facility with words, numbers, and logical reasoning. There are other capabilities that Gardner suggests deserve to be represented as intelligent behavior, including ability with music, images, nature, feelings, social interaction, and physical expertise. Once we embrace a model of intelligence that encompasses this more comprehensive rendering of the human mind, then the gifts of individuals with intellectual disabilities are more likely to be recognized, celebrated, and developed.

There are several different kinds of intellectual disabilities, each with its own unique pattern of gifts and abilities. One of the most common is Down syndrome, affecting more than 350,000 people in the United States (approximately 1 in every 800 births). It may surprise some readers to know that information about the strengths and abilities of those with Down syndrome goes all the way back to the doctor who discovered the syndrome in the mid-19th century. John Langdon Down wrote the following about children with Down syndrome: "They have considerable power of imitation, even bordering on being mimics. They are humorous, and a lively sense of the ridiculous often colors their mimicry. This faculty of imitation may be cultivated to a very great extent, and a practical direction given to the results obtained" (Down, 1866). More recently, psychologist Elizabeth M. Dykens has written about the social and personal strengths of people with Down syndrome:

> Persons with Down syndrome have been consistently cast as friendly and charming, with disarming smiles. Indeed, many toddlers and children with Down syndrome smile more often than their typically developing or mentally retarded peers . . . parents continue to spontaneously use upbeat, happy descriptors of their children. In this vein, several articulate young adults with Down syndrome have asked that their syndrome be renamed . . . "Up syndrome." (Dykens, 2006, p. 189)

One recent survey of nearly 300 persons with Down syndrome age 12 and older indicated that 99 percent were happy with their lives, 97 percent liked who they were, and 96 percent liked how they looked (Skotko, Levine, & Goldstein, 2011). Other studies have demonstrated that individuals with Down syndrome possess strong visual-motor skills (Wang, 1996) and well-developed nonverbal social interaction skills (Mundi, Sigman, Kasari, & Yirmiya, 1988), shared humor and laughter (Reddy, Williams, & Vaughan, 2001), and spatial short-term memory (Visu-Petra, Benga, Tincas, & Miclea, 2007).

People with Williams syndrome, by contrast, display a very different pattern of strengths. Williams syndrome is a rare form of intellectual disability that affects approximately 1 in every 10,000 births. Those affected have significant difficulty with logical-mathematical reasoning and spatial skills, but frequently show strengths in musical ability. Studies suggest, for example, that perfect pitch is more common among those with Williams syndrome than among the general population (Lenhoff, Perales, & Hickok, 2001) and that people with Williams syndrome rank higher in musical accomplishment, engagement, and interest when compared to control groups (Levitin et al., 2004). They also often display a flair for oral expression and frequently enjoy the company of other people (Lenhoff, Wang, Greenberg, & Bellugi, 1997).

Another category of intellectual disabilities, Fragile X syndrome, affects about 1 in 3,600 males and 1 in 4,000–6,000 females. Research suggests that, although the abstract reasoning abilities of those possessing this syndrome are severely compromised, they show strengths in the personal intelligences. According to Children's Hospital in Boston:

> Children with fragile X syndrome often have a good sense of humor, excellent memories, and great imitation skills. Although they may have social anxiety or shyness, they have a strong desire for social interactions and are often described as loving or sweet. People with fragile X syndrome often have a strong empathy for the feelings of others as well. (Children's Hospital Boston, 2005–2011)

Similarly, children with Willi-Prader syndrome (affecting approximately 1 in 15,000 births) have a strong nurturing streak manifested "in desires to work with babies, children, and animals" (Dykens, 2006, p. 189). They also enjoy reading and often have a remarkable ability to solve jigsaw and search-a-word puzzles.

Finally, individuals with fetal alcohol syndrome (a disorder that affects 1 in every 750 births) show strengths, interests, and abilities in some of the following areas: music, playing instruments, composing, singing, art, spelling, reading, computers, mechanics, woodworking, skilled vocations (e.g., welding, electrical work), writing, and poetry (Malbin, 2002).

Positive Role Models

The bright and shining lights among those with intellectual disabilities probably aren't going to turn into Einsteins, Picassos, or Mozarts, but that does not diminish their accomplishments one bit. Certainly the aforementioned actor and writer Jason Kingsley would qualify as a positive role model for those who have intellectual disabilities. So, too, would actor, author, and musician Chris Burke, who played Corky Thatcher on the TV show *Life Goes On*. He was the first person with Down syndrome to have a regular role on national television. As with Kingsley, Burke's parents were told by their obstetrician to put their baby in an institution when he was born, but his parents refused and instead focused on his innate abilities. As his mother observed: "He loved to perform for us, from the time he was very little. He was very musical. He had that talent early on. Before he actually verbalized, he was entertaining us" (Burke & McDaniel, 1991, p. 49).

In primary school, Burke loved to act out stories in the classroom. In junior high school, he frequently played leading roles in school plays. After high school, he took courses in filmmaking and improvisational theater at a private nonprofit agency serving adults with disabilities and wrote short TV scripts at home. He finally got his wish to perform on TV when Jason Kingsley's mother recommended him to a casting agent. Currently, he tours the country with his four-piece folk band, speaks at schools and nonprofit organizations, and serves as Goodwill Ambassador for the National Down Syndrome Society.

Other examples of positive role models among those with intellectual disabilities include the following individuals:

- Gloria Lenhoff, who has Williams syndrome and can sing opera in 25 different languages, including Chinese. (You can read about her life story in the 2006 book *The Strangest Song: One Father's Quest to Help His Daughter Find Her Voice*, by Teri Sforza, Howard Lenhoff, & Sylvia Lenhoff.)
- Sujeet Desai, who has Down syndrome and plays several instruments—including bass clarinet, alto saxophone, violin, piano, trumpet, and drums—and has a black belt in martial arts
- Katie Apostolides, who was the first person with Down syndrome to receive a formal degree from a credentialed college (an associate's degree in science)

- Jane Cameron, whose huge tapestries have been commissioned by such organizations as the office of the Prime Minister of Canada, Quebec's Mirabel Airport, and Reader's Digest Canada
- Bernadette Resha, whose paintings and drawings are exhibited in art galleries and art shows around the country
- Gretchen Josephson, writer and poet, whose 1997 book *Bus Girl* documents her daily life as she gains greater independent life skills
- Karen Gaffney, who successfully swam the English Channel when she was 23 as part of a six-person relay team
- Susan Harrington, one of the stars of an MTV weekly series about people with disabilities entitled *How's Your News?*

Another group of high achievers with intellectual disabilities are the athletes of the Special Olympics, which currently serves over 3 million people with intellectual disabilities from 180 countries in year-round training and competition. Standouts in this group include power weightlifter Jackie Barrett, who broke the Special Olympics record for the squat of 585 pounds, and golfer Scott Rohrer, who set the Special Olympics record for 18 holes of golf at 71. But of course, all the participants are champions. Research suggests that 52 percent of adult athletes who participate in the Special Olympics have jobs compared to 10 percent of all adults with intellectual disabilities, suggesting that participation has a formative role in helping them to achieve physical health, self-confidence, self-esteem, and socialization skills (Special Olympics, 2005).

Assistive Technologies/ Universal Design for Learning

Many of the assistive technologies and UDL approaches discussed in earlier chapters, especially those for children with learning disabilities and autism, are also appropriate for students with intellectual disabilities. These include word processors, calculators, books on tape, and especially the many apps available for computers, tablets, and smart phones. Reflecting on her 13-year-old son with Down syndrome, one mother noted:

> He's a wizard with the iPhone. He picked up his uncle's iPhone one day, and without anyone telling him how to do it, he found and figured out every game app on it (and there were a lot). The touch screen and the apps are intuitive to him in a way that a keyboard is not. My only gripe is that the screen is so small. So now comes the iPad, which is essentially an iPhone on steroids. (Dwight, 2010)

Augmentative and alternative communication (AAC) programs are particularly important for many students with intellectual disabilities who struggle with communication and articulation problems. The term *AAC* refers to all forms of communication other than oral speech used to express thoughts, desires, and needs. We all use AAC when we make facial expressions or gestures or use written symbols or pictures to communicate. Until recently, high-tech versions of AAC devices were, as one writer put it, "huge, heavy, and expensive." Now, however, with touch-screen tablets like the iPad, AAC apps are easy to use, highly portable, and relatively inexpensive. One good example is Proloquo2go, an iPad app consisting of onscreen picture buttons that represent different words, phrases, or sentences (e.g., "I need to go to the bathroom," "I'm hungry," "This is too hot"). When the appropriate button is pressed, the word, phrase, or sentence is synthesized into spoken language. There is a default vocabulary of over 7,000 items in Proloquo2go's digital library, and the device can be customized by typing in other words, phrases, or sentences that are converted to picture buttons. (This application is also very useful with many nonverbal autistic students.) Also helpful for students are apps that help them learn social, academic, and daily life tasks through video displays that can be replayed as often as necessary.

Another high-tech pathway that shows promise in helping students with intellectual disabilities learn new tasks is the emerging field of interactive mimetic digital game (IMDG) platforms such as Nintendo Wii and Microsoft Kinect for Xbox. These platforms allow players to engage in the physical motions of sports such as tennis, golf, bowling, billiards, or table tennis while holding onto or standing on sensors that translate their physical motions into actions on the computer screen. Some games even take players into fantasy worlds where they can run, fly, fight, or navigate their way through a wide range of adventures. Researchers at Nottingham Trent University's School of Education in the United Kingdom had high school participants with a variety of intellectual and developmental disabilities engage in tennis and bowling activities using Nintendo Wii and found that they improved not only their virtual game scores but also their real bowling and tennis scores. Moreover, 92 percent of the participants said they would like to use video games to help them learn in college in the future. As the key researcher, Rachel Folds, noted:

> The initial results from this small sample suggest that interactive games teach the students movements which they can improve upon and mimic in everyday life. Although they were playing tennis and bowling in the trial, games which teach them how to do things like bake a cake or change a tire could potentially be very beneficial. (Davison, 2011)

Other researchers have similarly found significant improvements in learning for students with intellectual disabilities when using a virtual reality platform (see, for example, Rahman & Rahman, 2010; Wuang, Chiang, Su, & Wang, 2011).

Enhanced Human Resources

Weaving a rich tapestry of human relations is very important for students with intellectual disabilities, who can frequently feel socially isolated and even victimized by bullying from fellow students (Norwich & Kelly, 2004). Although paraprofessionals are often invaluable in providing one-to-one support, especially where severe communication or mobility problems exist, there is some concern that these aides can further isolate students by overprotecting them or by failing to engage with them in a mutual give-and-take process (Broer, Doyle, & Giangreco, 2005). More important in terms of adult support is the quality of the students' relationships with both regular and special education teachers. Working together, these teachers can help support the students' experiences and maximize their opportunities for success in the classroom.

It's also vital that students with intellectual disabilities establish positive and supportive relationships with their peers (both those with disabilities and those who are neurotypical). Programs exist to facilitate such relationships, including Best Buddies and Circles of Friends, and should be instituted whenever possible. Other opportunities for meaningful peer interaction need to be pursued as well, including the use of cooperative learning, group discussions, social games, mutual reading, lab partnerships, homework buddies, extracurricular activities (e.g., sports, choir), and peer tutoring. Studies suggest that students with intellectual disabilities can even benefit from serving as tutors themselves, to both neurodiverse and neurotypical peers, on such topics as vocabulary, reading, social studies, math, spelling, and sign language (Spencer & Balboni, 2003).

Educators should also make use of the human resources available in the wider community. There are many organizations that help students with intellectual disabilities develop their creative abilities. For high school students with intellectual disabilities who are engaged in vocational or occupational training, a job coach can be an invaluable mediator with their coworkers and employers by training, monitoring, assessing, and supporting the students as they become more confident and effective in their work roles.

Strength-Based Learning Strategies

The most important thing to keep in mind when working with students who have intellectual disabilities is that they learn best from instruction that is experiential, vivid, hands-on, and down-to-earth. Overly verbal, highly abstract, and unnecessarily complex explanations and instructions are to be avoided. (Of course, this teaching philosophy applies to all learners.) We've already seen that students with intellectual disabilities often show strengths in musical, spatial, interpersonal, and kinesthetic intelligences. Educators should emphasize these intelligences whenever possible when developing instructional strategies. Instead of giving students paper-and-pencil math word problems, for example, teachers would be better advised to put on a puppet show in which the puppets act out the word problems.

Teaching through games is another strategy that can benefit students with intellectual disabilities. When studying vocabulary words, for example, instead of simply providing words and definitions from a textbook, have students play a "Chutes and Ladders"–type board game using markers and dice. When students land on squares, they have to provide the meaning of the vocabulary word given. Make learning hands-on at every opportunity. Instead of lecturing on the three states of matter (solid, liquid, gas), for example, provide a laboratory experiment where an ice cube is dissolved into water and then boiled into steam.

Engage students by linking lessons to their personal lives and by using interesting artifacts whenever possible. When lecturing on the skeletal system, for example, ask the students if they've ever broken or bruised any bones in their body, and use a life-sized model of a human skeleton as a learning tool. Make learning activities project based. When studying geography and maps, for example, help the students create a highly visual and colorful map of their journey from home to school or to a friend's house. Use memory mnemonics that employ music, acronyms, pictures, physical activities, or stories.

To learn spelling words, for example, have the students sing any seven-letter word to the tune of "Twinkle Twinkle Little Star," or any three-letter words to the tune of "Three Blind Mice." Use Chisanbop (Korean finger math) or other tactile methods for doing mathematical calculations.

Because many students with intellectual disabilities have strengths in drama and imitation, use role play and improvisation to teach new material. After reading a story, for example, have the students play the role of the main characters and dramatize the action of the plot. Or, in learning U.S. history, show them how to act out the roles of significant figures in the Civil War, such as Abraham Lincoln and Ulysses S. Grant. When teaching subjects that involve sequences, show students how to draw a storyboard or comic strip of the significant sequence of events in a book they are reading.

Other instructional strategies for use with students with intellectual disabilities include the following:

- Use real-life experiences as opportunities to learn (e.g., setting up audiovisual equipment, landscaping, providing office help).

- Employ self-paced learning materials (including software for computer, tablet, or smart phone) that allow students to work through academic skills at their own level, receive immediate feedback, and make steady progress.

- Be dramatic when presenting new learning material (e.g., show enthusiasm, use props, dress up in costume).

- Develop the students' emotional intelligence by asking them to reflect on their feelings (e.g., frustration, excitement, boredom) as they learn something new.

- Teach the same concept in many different contexts so that the learning becomes generalized (e.g., point out the use of vocabulary words whenever they're spoken during the day).

- Listen carefully to what students say (or, if they are nonverbal, pay attention to how they express themselves), and use the students' own words, ideas, and behaviors to help move the curriculum forward.

- Integrate music into the curriculum (e.g., in history, teach Civil War–era songs; in literature, play music that serves as a background to a story or play).

Affirmative Career Aspirations

Helping students with intellectual disabilities to envision positive career pathways is critical in preparing them for successful and fulfilling lives. Only 15 percent of families report that their adult family members with intellectual or developmental disabilities are employed in any capacity either part-time or full-time (The Arc, 2011). Unfortunately, individuals with intellectual disabilities have a long history of low expectations from others when it comes to work roles. H. H. Goddard, the psychologist who coined the term "moron" to describe people with an IQ score between 51 and 70, wrote in 1919 that people with intellectual disabilities "do a great deal of work that no one else will do. . . . There is an immense amount of drudgery to be done, an immense amount of work for which we do not wish to pay enough to secure more intelligent workers" (quoted in Calavita, 2010, p. 52). Even as recently as a couple of decades ago, individual with intellectual disabilities were thought to be only capable of work that involved what were called the four *F*s: *food* (washing dishes), *flowers* (gardening and yard work), *folding* (napkins in restaurants or sheets as chambermaids), and *filth* (custodial work) (Sforza et al., 2006).

Still today, too many workers with intellectual disabilities, earning subminimum wages, labor in "sheltered workshops" where they engage in repetitive tasks such as assembling boxes or stuffing envelopes under close supervision (National Disability Rights Network, 2010). Thankfully, over the last decade, thinking has changed regarding appropriate employment for people with intellectual disabilities. "We've moved away from the concept that people with these disabilities are only suited to dishwashing, cleaning, and that sort of thing," says William Kiernan, director of the Institute for Community Inclusion at the University of Massachusetts in Boston. "At our institute, we have a couple of folks with intellectual disabilities who are doing data collection for us" (Andrews, 2005).

Other work roles that people with intellectual disabilities have successfully engaged in include the following:

- Animal caretaker
- Library assistant
- Mail clerk
- Store clerk
- Messenger
- Cook
- Printer
- Cashier
- Medical technician
- Furniture refinisher
- Photocopier operator
- Grocery clerk
- Sales clerk
- Hospital attendant
- Automobile detail worker
- Clerical aide

In addition to these careers, some individuals with intellectual disabilities have managed to successfully become entrepreneurs, often starting businesses that are artistic in nature. Examples include professional photographer Clara Link; the musician Sujeet Desai, who travels extensively to perform in local, national, and international events; watercolor artist Ruth Tonack, whose paintings sell at a local store and whose art has taken her as far away as Germany; and the Famous People Players, a black-light puppetry company that employs people with physical and intellectual disabilities.

Research suggests that people with intellectual disabilities are often more energetic and reliable in their work roles than typically developing individuals. A three-year study at a major U.S. financial firm, for example, found a turnover rate of 8 percent for individuals with developmental disabilities compared with an overall rate of 45 percent for typically developing adults (Life Skills, 2009). One key to helping individuals find appropriate employment in adulthood involves getting them engaged in thinking about and preparing for employment while they are still in school. Project SEARCH, for example, prepares high school seniors with intellectual and developmental disabilities by giving them vocational training for part of the day and having them work as interns at different federal agencies learning skills that prepare them for future employment (Project SEARCH, 2011–2012). Many postsecondary programs are also available for individuals with intellectual disabilities, with nearly 200 college-based programs providing a combination of academic, social, and vocational instruction. One recent study suggested that youth with intellectual disabilities who participated in postsecondary education were 26 percent more likely than those with no postsecondary education experience to leave vocational rehabilitation services with a paid job and earn a 73 percent higher weekly income (112th Cong., 2011).

Environmental Modifications

Researchers at the New Jersey Institute of Technology's Center for Architecture and Building Research recently made recommendations for modifying school environments to benefit individuals with intellectual disabilities. They suggested placing way-finding aids around the school, including landmarks, color-coded doors and halls, and the repetition of visual, auditory, and tactile signs, cues, and patterns to enable students to navigate the building and feel more secure in it (Hutchings & Olsen, 2008). It can also be helpful to have photographs and pictures in the classroom to designate specific functions and tasks—for example, a photo of how to properly use the water fountain, or pictures to indicate what is stored inside each storage unit in class.

Scenario #1: Brittany

Brittany is a 10-year-old who has been diagnosed as having fetal alcohol syndrome. She performs below grade level in all her subjects except art and physical education. She works hard but can be very tough on herself when things don't go well, even to the point of being verbally self-abusive. She is socially isolated because of her controlling behaviors toward others, and she responds to rejection by being physically aggressive with her classmates. She has difficulty remembering and following even simple instructions, and she will often leave out key details when retelling a story. She also has significant problems with higher-order thinking tasks.

Poor Niche Construction

Britanny is placed in a special class for all her subjects. She is assigned for part of the day to a newly hired paraprofessional without special training who treats her like a much younger child and doesn't expect much from her academically. Brittany throws tantrums when she doesn't get her way and spends a good portion of the day in the time-out area in a corner of the special education classroom. Her classmates bully her for having an "alkie" mother and call her "retard" and "crack baby" to her face. As a result, she frequently gets into fights on the playground. She spends most of her time in class doing primary-level worksheets, which she often doodles on and sometimes turns into little origami structures, for which she is reprimanded.

Positive Niche Construction

Britanny is fully included in the regular 5th grade classroom and is assigned a volunteer "study buddy" from the Gifted and Talented program to help her with her reading and math homework. A survey of her strengths and interests indicates that Britanny loves to draw, play the piano, knit, play softball, and collect dolls. She is appointed as an "artist in residence" in art class to help other kids with their drawing and painting skills, and she puts on a show of her own hand-knitted dolls' clothing, which is displayed prominently in the school lobby. She is named assistant captain of the 5th grade girls' softball team, where her controlling behaviors turn out to be an asset in directing the flow of the game. To help her with following directions in class, she is given an iPad and uses the application Stories2Learn, which she uses to put together personalized narratives of social situations that she needs to master using text, photos, and audio prompts. To help with her reading skills, Britanny uses the FastForWord software program, which she enjoys using because it allows her to move through the program at her own pace. She also plays problem-solving video games to help develop her higher-order thinking skills.

Scenario #2: Phillip

Phillip is a 16-year-old boy with Down syndrome and an IQ score of 60. He currently does math at a 1st grade level and reads at a 2nd grade level. He has mild articulation problems which are exacerbated by stress, and as a result he is sometimes not understood by his teacher or classmates and has to repeat things, causing him additional frustration. He usually spends his recess and lunch periods by himself or with a student who has fragile X syndrome. He sometimes gets into trouble with the teacher for acting silly in class and has to be disciplined. He has vision problems and has been fitted with corrective lenses. He also has fine-motor difficulties, particularly when it comes to holding a pencil, which he grips with his whole fist. As a result, his writing is often messy and smeared. He is moderately obese and physically awkward, and is frequently laughed at by the boys in physical education class.

Poor Niche Construction

Phillip has spent his entire school career in a self-contained special education program with other kids who have been deemed "educable mentally retarded." He is often called "retarded" by kids in the regular classes, who derisively imitate his slurred speech. As a consequence, he suffers bouts of low self-esteem and depression. He spends much of his time in class doing remedial worksheets and workbooks in reading and math, and he is awarded points for every worksheet he successfully completes (he trades in the points at the end of the week for special prizes like cookies or other snacks, which contribute to his obesity problem). His teacher yells at him for his poor penmanship and has given him a penmanship workbook to complete, but otherwise no attempt has been made to help him write more neatly. He sees a physical therapist once a week to work on coordination and balance activities, which he must do outdoors in plain sight of several regular classrooms. When he acts silly in class, his teacher criticizes his "baby behavior" and has on more than one occasion brought in Gerber's baby food to give to him in front of the other students as a way of humiliating him into acting more mature.

Positive Niche Construction

Phillip is fully included in the regular classroom for all subjects. He spends a good deal of time working at a computer terminal alongside his typically developing classmates on academic material that is adjusted for his reading and math levels. He reads books on the same topics as his classmates, but at an appropriate reading level, using either books on tape or interactive digital books. He also uses a talking calculator in math class. Phillip expresses pride in the fact that he is taking the same courses as his typically developing peers. He has a real gift for imitating others and for expressing deep emotion, and uses this gift in history class, where he has taken on such diverse roles as a farmer during the Great Depression and a Pilgrim crossing the Atlantic Ocean. He has appeared in several school theatrical presentations and has begun taking acting lessons after school at a local community service center for people with disabilities. He is well liked by his classmates, who have given him the nickname "Corky" after the role played by Chris Burke on the TV show *Life Goes On*, which his teacher has played for the class as a way of highlighting the accomplishments of people with disabilities. He uses a pencil grip, which has helped him with his handwriting, and he's been using Proloquo2go on the iPad to type in customized sentences that he then "speaks" in class (and in some of the school plays). As a result, he is more easily understood.

Sample Strategies for Applying Positive Niche Construction to Common Core State Standards

Sample Standard: K.CC.6—Identify whether the number of objects in one group is greater than, less than, or equal to the number of objects in another group, e.g., by using counting and matching strategies (include groups with up to 10 objects).

Strength Awareness

Discover the student's strongest means of expression (e.g., verbal, visual, tactile/kinesthetic, musical, social) and employ this modality in learning the standard. If the student is a tactile/kinesthetic learner, for example, let her respond by using gestures to indicate "more," "less," and "equal" or by touching pictures that symbolize these concepts.

Positive Role Models

Videotape a neurotypical student of about the student's same age who successfully completes this standard, and show the video to the neurodiverse student.

Assistive Technologies/Universal Design for Learning

- If the student is nonverbal or has difficulty with articulation, let him use augmented and alternative communication software (e.g., Proloquo2go) to respond to prompts.
- Use an early math software program that teaches the concepts of "more," "less," and "equal." Have the student do problems and receive immediate feedback (e.g., flashing lights, bright music) for his correct responses.

Enhanced Human Resources

- Group the student with other children engaged in this standard to enable her to learn from their experiences.
- Assign a peer tutor to help the student with the standard.

Strength-Based Learning Strategies

- Engage the student's personal interests to support the standard. If the student loves to play with miniature soldiers, for example, use them in groups to illustrate "more," "less," and "equal."
- Encourage the student to touch each object as she counts. If the student has not yet mastered counting to 10, work on this objective before teaching the standard.
- Make up a story in which a hero has to determine whether one group of individuals is greater than, equal to, or less than another group of people.
- Use the student's classmates as "objects" (e.g., by separating them into two groups and having the student determine whether one group is greater than, equal to, or less than the other group).

Affirmative Career Aspirations

Have the student count and compare groups of coins. This practice can prepare the student to become comfortable with money—a necessity for any future job in which counting and comparing money is required.

Environmental Modifications

Determine the context in which the student is most secure and comfortable (e.g., outdoors, near a sandbox, at a table with a rubber ball chair, at his own desk, on the floor), and carry out the counting and comparing activity in that preferred setting.

Assessing the Standard

Using pointing and matching strategies initiated by teacher prompts in a setting that the student is comfortable with and employing an augmentative communication device if needed, the student will indicate whether one group of no more than 10 objects that he has personally selected is more than, less than, or equal to another group of the same objects.

Conclusion

As the saying goes, it is not how intelligent you are, but how you are intelligent. Once we begin to understand this maxim, we can start to fundamentally transform our perspectives of students with intellectual disabilities. Although the logical and linguistic abilities of most individuals with intellectual disabilities have been compromised, other intelligences—including musical, spatial, naturalist, bodily/kinesthetic, and inter- and intrapersonal—may have been spared and thus represent opportunities for the student to feel confident and succeed in schoolwork. As IQ testing begins to recede in importance, we can start to appreciate these individuals in a new way. For too long, people with intellectual disabilities have been the object of what I like to call "neurobigotry." They've been called "retarded" and ridiculed for looking or acting differently from the rest of the crowd. Let's honor and celebrate their different ways of thinking and learning. This can only serve to support them in their aspirations to become successful members of society.

For Further Study

1. **Create a unit on "Heroes with Intellectual Disabilities."** Every week or month, showcase with a photo and biography a particular individual with intellectual disabilities who has achieved success in a given area (e.g., graduated from college, won an event at the Special Olympics, created a work of art). What happens when students with and without disabilities learn that a person with intellectual disabilities can do amazing things?

2. **Investigate the concept of intelligence. Study Howard Gardner's theory of multiple intelligences (see his book *Frames of Mind,* for example, or my book, *Multiple Intelligences in the Classroom,* 3rd edition).** Learn about the checkered history of IQ testing by reading Stephen J. Gould's *The Mismeasure of Man.* For a contrasting point of view, look at Richard Herrnstein and Charles Murray's *The Bell Curve.* How do your own beliefs about intelligence affect your attitudes toward people with intellectual disabilities?

3. **Get involved in the campaign to put an end to use of the word *retarded* and replace it with the term *intellectual disabilities*.** (Go to www.r-word.org for more information.) How has "the 'r' word" been used in your school? What steps might you take to replace it with the term *intellectual disabilities*?

(Continued on next page)

For Further Study *(Continued)*

4. Develop a curriculum plan for one or more students with intellectual disabilities that allows them to study the same topic as their typically developing peers, but at their own level of ability. What assistive technologies/ UDL approaches can you use to help facilitate this plan? What sorts of texts, materials, and differentiated learning strategies might you utilize?

5. Look into options for vocational training and post-secondary education available in your community for middle and high school students. (Go to www .thinkcollege.net for more information.) Fan the fires of the career aspirations of elementary-aged children with intellectual disabilities by regularly discussing possible careers. Invite employed individuals with intellectual disabilities to come in and talk about their jobs. Engage your high school students with intellectual disabilities in sharing what they'd like to do when they graduate, and set up internships, apprenticeships, and other real-life activities that can help prepare them for adult life.

6. Create a "Best Buddies" or "Circles of Friends" program in your school that pairs individuals with intellectual or developmental disabilities with neurotypical peers. (Go to www.bestbuddies.org or www.circleoffriends.org for more information.) Alternatively, include students with intellectual disabilities in meaningful social interactions with typically developing peers through cooperative learning, group discussions, or peer tutoring. What effect do these practices have on students with intellectual disabilities in terms of their self-concept, class acceptance, academic progress, and social skills? What effect do these practices have on neurotypical students who engage in them?

7. **Invite representatives from organizations for people with intellectual disabilities to visit your school and discuss the challenges and promises of living with these disabilities.** For example, if you have a student with Down syndrome, ask the National Association for Down Syndrome to send a representative to discuss the ups and downs of living with the condition. Other organizations might include the Williams Syndrome Association, National Fragile X Foundation, National Organization on Fetal Alcohol Syndrome, Prader-Willi Syndrome Association, International Rett Syndrome Association, or the American Association of Intellectual and Developmental Disabilities. What effect do these visits have on the attitudes of both your intellectually disabled and typically developing students toward people with intellectual disabilities?

6 | The Bright Side of Kids with Emotional and Behavioral Disorders

A person needs a little madness, or else they never dare cut the rope and be free.

—*Nikos Kazantzakis, writer*

There is something uniquely problematic about students with emotional and behavioral disorders. They fail more classes, earn lower grade point averages, miss more days of school, and are retained more than students with other disabilities. Half of all students with emotional and behavioral disorders drop out of school—the highest rate for any disability category. Twenty percent are arrested before they even leave school (Lewis, Jones, Horner, & Sugai, 2010). Only 25 percent of public school teachers believe students with emotional and behavioral disorders should be included in the regular classroom (Howell, West, & Peterson, 2008), and only 30 percent of these students *are* fully included. The majority are in special classrooms, special schools, or residential facilities (Danforth & Morris, 2006). Once placed in special education programs, fewer than 10 percent will ever return full-time to regular classrooms. Perhaps the most astonishing statistic of all is that while an estimated 9 to 19 percent of all school-age children meet the criteria for emotional or behavioral disorders, fewer than 1 percent of them have actually been identified and are receiving special education services (Heathfield & Clark, 2004). Former school administrator Mary Beth Hewett writes:

> Out of all of the disabilities, mental illness is the last to come out of the disability "closet." You don't see poster children for [emotional disorders]. Although rough estimates indicate that one in five individuals will have some form of emotional illness in their lifetime, it is still the disability that very few talk about. (Hewitt, 2005)

Although the above statistics are sobering, there is another, brighter dimension to students with emotional and behavioral disorders that is rarely publicized: namely, their intrinsic gifts and abilities. In the years I spent teaching kids with learning problems and emotional and behavioral disorders, I was constantly challenged and often aggravated by my students' difficult behaviors. At the same time, I was frequently surprised and delighted by their insights, charisma, playfulness, and vitality. Polly, the stressed-out 8-year-old daughter of a high-level business executive, would select puppets during her recess, line them up, and begin teaching them using some of the same mannerisms that I and her other teachers employed. Eric, a 9-year-old who was the victim of physical abuse at home—he told me his father had attacked him with a hammer—would create clay houses and then rig them up with battery-powered electrical circuits to provide indoor lighting: a haven of domestic safety for him. Jacob, a grimy 9-year-old who had been abandoned by his family and periodically left to roam in nature, often used original language to express himself. (I still use his word for a staple remover—*jabberjaws*—when I'm busy doing office work.) These kids glowed with a terrible but powerful light. Their traumas and personal demons often worked together with their charisma to help forge their unforgettable personalities.

Strengths Awareness

Throughout history, great thinkers have often made the connection between mental illness and creativity or high achievement. Aristotle once asked, "Why is it that all those who have become eminent in philosophy or politics or poetry or the arts are clearly of an atrabilious [melancholic] temperament?" (quoted in Forster, 1927). Edgar Allan Poe, who himself suffered from an emotional disorder, wrote semibiographically:

> Men have called me mad; but the question is not yet settled, whether madness is or is not the loftiest intelligence —whether much that is glorious—whether all that is profound—does not spring from disease of thought—from moods of mind exalted at the expense of the general intellect. (Poe, 1850/2004, p. 1)

More recently, Johns Hopkins University professor Kay Redfield Jamison, in her book *Touched with Fire: Manic Depressive Illness and the Artistic Temperament,* drew from the lives of artists such as Vincent Van Gogh, Lord Byron, and Virginia Woolf to examine the links between bipolar disorder (BD) and creativity (Jamison, 1996). Her path-finding work received empirical verification in 2005 when researchers at Stanford University gave creativity tests to parents and children with BD and compared them to control groups. Children with BD scored higher on tests of figural (pictorial) creativity than matched controls. The coauthors of the study wrote:

> This is the first study to show that children with and at high risk for BD have higher creativity than healthy control children. The finding in children and in adults was related to an

enhanced ability to experience and express dislike of simple and symmetric images. This could reflect increased access to negative affect, which could yield both benefits with respect to providing affective energy for creative achievement, but also yield liabilities with respect to quality of interpersonal relationships or susceptibility to depression. (Simeonova, Chang, Strong, & Ketter, 2005, p. 623)

Positive Role Models

As noted above, many famous individuals, especially in the arts and humanities, have had some form of emotional or behavioral disorder. Psychologist Arnold Ludwig surveyed over 1,000 eminent individuals of the 20th century and discovered that 77 percent of poets, 54 percent of fiction writers, 50 percent of visual artists, and 46 percent of composers had undergone at least one significant depressive episode in their lives (Ludwig, 1995).

As Figure 6.1 shows, emotional and behavioral disorders aren't limited to those in the arts. Astonishingly, *almost half* of American presidents from 1789 to 1974—including Abraham Lincoln, Ulysses S. Grant, Theodore Roosevelt, and Calvin Coolidge—suffered from mental illness sometime during their lives, according to an analysis by psychiatrists at Duke University Medical Center (Carey, 2006). Another prominent statesman with mental illness was Winston Churchill, who referred to his depression as his "black dog." Today, in the entertainment business, there are numerous examples of famous personalities who are battling emotional disorders, from Woody Allen's anxiety disorder and Angelina Jolie's bipolar disorder to Brooke Shields's postpartum depression and Barbra Streisand's panic attacks. Many well-known entertainers have broken new ground by making these disorders more visible in the culture, thus creating heightened awareness that brings with it greater acceptance and an increase in proper identification and treatment for millions of people. Students

6.1 Notable Individuals with Emotional and Behavioral Disorders	
The Arts	Jackson Pollock, Robert Schumann, Vincent Van Gogh, Michelangelo, Joan Miró
The Sciences	John Nash, J. Robert Oppenheimer, Friedrich August Hayek, Julian Huxley, Isaac Newton
Business	John D. Rockefeller, T. Boone Pickens Jr., Ted Turner, Donald Trump, Philip Graham
Entertainment	Britney Spears, Ben Stiller, Angelina Jolie, Owen Wilson, Brooke Shields
Sports	Ken Griffey Jr., Jerry West, Terry Bradshaw, Daryl Strawberry, Mike Tyson
Politics & The Military	Winston Churchill, Abraham Lincoln, Boris Yeltsin, Calvin Coolidge, Theodore Roosevelt
Writers	J. K. Rowling, Emily Dickinson, William Faulkner, Leo Tolstoy, Walt Whitman

might select one or more of these notable individuals and design a multimedia presentation to share with the class, emphasizing how they managed to cope with their disability while engaging in creative pursuits or other forms of achievement.

Assistive Technologies/ Universal Design for Learning

I once had a student in my classroom who threw periodic tantrums when he didn't get his way. One day, I took a photograph of him in the midst of one of his outbursts, and when he had calmed down, I showed him the picture. His jaw dropped as he looked at it. He had never seen himself portrayed in this way before. After that, he never threw a tantrum in class again.

As this story suggests, technology can be a great asset in helping students with emotional and behavior disorders take more responsibility for their learning and behavior. One strategy is to take photographs—or, better yet, video—of a student behaving both appropriately and inappropriately. Then show the student both scenarios and discuss the differences. This approach can help many individuals with behavior and emotional disorders understand more clearly what is expected of them in the classroom (Blood, Johnson, Ridenour, Simmons, & Crouch, 2011). Also useful are self-monitoring strategies, whereby a student selects a target behavior or learning goal, inputs into a spreadsheet or a database, and then keeps track of his progress on a smart phone, tablet, or computer (Sutherland & Snyder, 2007). The smart phone app TraxItAll, for example, is one database application that can be used for this purpose. Another good self-monitoring application is the T2 Mood Tracker, which allows the user to keep track of his emotions and anxieties over an extended period of time and thus get a better handle on his emotional life. Cumming (2010) shows how students with emotional or behavioral disorders can create computer-based multimedia presentations that enhance their motivation and engagement in school. Finally, any self-paced learning program that provides immediate feedback and that challenges the student without frustrating him can help reduce the chances of conflict between student and teacher.

Enhanced Human Resources

The single-most important ingredient in positive niche construction for students with behavioral and emotional disorders is the provision of a nurturing network of supportive human beings who can champion and promote their students' emotional well-being and appropriate behavior. A team approach is essential. Teachers (both regular and special education) should collaborate with highly trained instructional assistants, mental health professionals, administrators, the school nurse, community agencies, and the students' families to create what has been called a "wraparound" approach to meeting the unique needs of each individual student (Suter & Bruns, 2009). This wraparound team serves to support the development of academic and social skills, social and family services, counseling or psychological therapy, and, when necessary, pharmacological treatment. The team can be especially helpful when issues such as child abuse, alcohol and drug abuse, lack of suitable housing, bullying, and other issues interfere with the student's ability to function effectively in the classroom.

Within the classroom itself, the teacher needs to create a positive learning environment with clear expectations for behavior, clearly communicated procedures (e.g., what to do if a pencil breaks), well-designed transitions (e.g., what to do when you're finished with your work), and fairly implemented consequences for both appropriate and inappropriate behavior. An especially important strategy for teachers is to frequently offer students specific and immediate praise as well as opportunities to respond in order to keep them engaged with the content of the lesson (Niesyn, 2009). Studies show that teachers rarely do this with students who have emotional and behavioral disorders, but that they can learn to do this more often if they regularly monitor their own teaching styles (Kalis, Vannest, & Parker, 2007; Salmon, 2006).

Teachers should also work to establish positive rapport with students who have emotional and behavioral disorders. One quick way to do this is to personally greet students at the door of the classroom, ask them about their day, and give them a "heads up" about what will occur during class that day. We should also remember that the students' own peers represent a wonderful human resource for helping them both academically and behaviorally. Research suggests that peer-assisted learning strategies, reciprocal peer tutoring, and classwide peer tutoring all help students with emotional and behavioral disorders succeed in the classroom (see, for example, Bowman-Perrott, 2009).

Strength-Based Learning Strategies

Teaching strategies for students with emotional and behavioral disorders include reinforcing positive behavior, employing frequent praise and encouragement, and providing students with regular feedback. Teachers should also show students how to monitor their own behavior over the course of the school day. This approach has been shown to enhance academic and social outcomes for students with emotional and behavioral disorders (Fitzpatrick & Knowlton, 2009). Teachers can help students pinpoint selected behaviors to observe (e.g., the number of times per day that they leave their seat without permission) and then assist them in the process of self-recording these behaviors when they occur. Often, the self-recording is enough to bring negative behaviors to a halt. As noted above, assistive technologies using computer, tablet, or smart phone apps can also be invaluable in carrying out the self-monitoring process.

Teaching self-talk skills has also been found to be a successful evidence-based intervention for students with emotional and behavioral disorders (Niesyn, 2009). Self-talk usually takes the form of "thinking out loud" through the steps of a given activity or assignment. So, for example, students might ask themselves, "Do I understand what I'm working on?" or "What don't I understand?" in order to organize their thinking about the assignment. Students can also use this approach to transform negative self-talk (e.g., "I'm a lousy student") into positive self-talk (e.g., "I succeed when I work hard"). Programs designed to help students become more "mindful" of their thinking processes and more positive in developing "learned optimism" have been shown to significantly reduce symptoms of depression and anxiety (Gillham et al., 2006), as have relaxation techniques to reduce stress (Goldbeck & Schmid, 2003; Lopata, Nida, & Marable, 2006). Teachers might also encourage their students to develop specific behavioral, academic, or personal goals (e.g., "I will get a *B* in History,"

"I will succeed in getting a part-time job") and support them as they take practical steps to achieve their objectives (see Byrne, 2008).

Students with emotional and behavioral disorders need to have regular opportunities to express their feelings through the arts using media such as painting, drawing, collage, clay, dramatic improvisation, music, puppetry, or dance. I cannot stress this enough, and it pains me to note that there is so little research on the use of expressive arts in educational settings with students who have emotional and behavioral disorders (see Hipsky, 2007; Rosal, 1993). (As an aside, if someone is looking for a good topic for a master's thesis or doctoral dissertation, I would recommend this area as a focus.)

Some years ago, I co-led an arts resource room for a summer program catering to kids with a wide range of special needs, including emotional and behavioral disorders. We discovered that the students who were causing the most havoc in their academic classes would enter the arts resource room and immediately become totally absorbed in the activity of the day, whether it was mask making, carpentry, clay modeling, or some other artistic project. All kids need to express themselves artistically, but this is even more important for those who struggle with their emotions and behavior.

It may also be helpful for students with emotional and behavioral disorders to keep a daily journal of their thoughts, feelings, dreams, goals, and aspirations in words and images. This journal should not be graded or marked up with red ink; rather, it should be a special protected place where students can let off steam and explore their feelings without having to act them out in the classroom (see Capacchione, 2008).

Here are a number of other strength-based learning strategies that can be useful with students who have emotional and behavioral disorders:

- Create a behavior contract co-created and signed by the student, the teacher, and the parent that includes positive goals, a set span of time for reaching them, and contingencies decided upon in advance by all signatories.

- Use a handheld microphone to amplify your voice and provide opportunities for students to ask questions, tell stories, present reports, and share projects.

- Hold class meetings during which all students have a chance to express feelings, solve problems, and generate solutions for running an efficient and positive classroom.

- Train students in peer mediation to manage disputes involving classmates.

- Use role play to model different solutions that occur in the classroom.

- Provide students with choices in reading materials, homework assignments, school-related projects, and other aspects of the curriculum.

- Give students meaningful responsibilities to carry out in the classroom or school (e.g., working in the principal's office, shadowing the custodian, helping the cafeteria workers).

- Use Life Space Crisis Intervention to deal with emotional meltdowns, aggression, depression, and other emotional problems that directly affect the classroom environment (go to www .lsci.org for more information).

Affirmative Career Aspirations

A review of the strengths of students with emotional and behavioral disorders suggests that some of these individuals might well be suited to careers in the arts, entertainment, or the humanities—or possibly even politics! More realistically, however, as noted at the beginning of this chapter, half of all students with emotional and behavioral disorders drop out of school before graduation, which hampers their ability to obtain gainful employment. Among those who do graduate, data from several longitudinal studies reveal that they experience longer delays in gaining employment and lower employment rates overall than the general population, and that they are also more likely to have several short-term jobs or part-time jobs and earn lower salaries than individuals with other disabilities (Jolivette, Stichter, Nelson, Scott, & Liaupsin, 2000). It is therefore imperative that students with emotional and behavioral disorders receive appropriate vocational guidance while they are still in school.

Of particular importance for students with emotional and behavioral disorders is the development of self-determination skills (Carter, Lane, Pierson, & Glaeser, 2006). Students need help developing their ability to understand and communicate their own strengths, set and work toward self-selected goals, advocate for themselves, and self-assess their own progress and outcomes. Instruction in self-determination skills should begin in the early grades and include all students, not just those with disabilities (Wehmeyer & Field, 2007).

Students also benefit from having positive role models from the community who had emotional or behavioral difficulties visit the school and discuss their own career paths. At the high school level, students should engage in vocational training (e.g., internships, apprenticeships, job shadowing) and meet in support groups to help articulate career goals, work on social skills necessary in the workplace, and discuss problems that may come up in the course of their employment. Above all, students need to develop their sense of self-efficacy and feel a sense of personal power (Stuart, 2003).

Environmental Modifications

Students with emotional and behavioral disorders require a structured, positive, and predictable environment, not only in the classroom but also in the hallways, in the cafeteria, on the playground, and in other educational settings. Researchers at the New Jersey Institute of Technology investigating the impact of school and classroom environments on inclusion found that buildings that were predictable, consistent, and orderly had a calming effect on students with behavioral issues and helped them focus on their work (Hutchings & Olsen, 2008). Placing students with emotional and behavioral disorders in an inclusive learning environment whenever possible allows them to interact regularly with typically developing peers and thus benefit from positive role models to help regulate their own behaviors, attitudes, and academic performance. Such a program, however, must have adequate institutional supports including the use of coteaching, where regular and special education teachers work together to meet students' individual needs (McDuffie, Landrum, & Gelman, 2008).

When evaluating students, it's helpful to consider the total learning environment in understanding what particular factors may be influencing their positive and negative behaviors. Such factors may include seating arrangements, the time of day when problem behaviors tend to manifest themselves, reactions to foods or medications, personal issues from outside school that spill into the classroom, and the presence or lack of opportunities for physical activity and positive social interactions. It's important to have a dedicated space, either in the classroom or somewhere else in the school, where students with emotional and behavioral disorders can retreat to when in crisis mode to regain self-control. Student and teacher should discuss beforehand where the space is going to be situated and what the criteria will be for going to the space. In many cases, the student should be allowed to initiate the time-out himself when he decides that he needs to get away from the turmoil and calm himself down. Above all, the space should not be considered as a punitive environment, but rather as a positive, even therapeutic, location for transmuting negative energies into positive behaviors and attitudes (see Nelsen, 1999).

Scenario #1: Bobby

Bobby is an 8th grader who has difficulties with self-control and aggression. If not constantly monitored, he pushes younger and weaker students around. He also has a problem with swearing and verbally abusing his peers in class. He complains that nobody likes him and that he gets picked on by his peers. If he gets into a fight, he invariably accuses the other person of starting it. His academic work is slightly below average. He reads at grade level and enjoys math, history, and Spanish. There is a history of physical abuse in his home, and social work agencies have become involved.

Poor Niche Construction

Bobby is placed part-time in a special education classroom for boys with behavior problems. As a result of the school's "zero tolerance" policy, Bobby spends much of his time sitting in the office. He has been suspended from school several times for fighting and swearing in both the regular and special education classrooms. The suspensions have led him to fall behind in his academic work, even though work is sent home on each occasion. In the teachers' lounge, Bobby's teachers regularly share "war stories" of their confrontations with him, and several suggest that he may not pass their course because of unfinished work, even though he appears to understand the material that is being presented. The school counselor (who is in school only one day a week) has yet to set up a meeting with Bobby.

Positive Niche Construction

Bobby is placed full-time in an inclusive classroom but is told that when he feels out of control, he can go to the "chill-out" room down the hall. A paraprofessional with experience teaching students with emotional and behavioral disorders usually accompanies Bobby to the crisis room to help him with his academic work, suggest ways to handle interpersonal conflicts with his peers, and teach him stress-reduction techniques to use when he feels anxious or stressed out. In the course of their discussions, Bobby reveals his love of baseball, comic books, and fishing. The assistant relays this information to Bobby's teachers, who integrate his interests into his regular academic work. Bobby is asked to tutor some of his classmates in math and Spanish. Regular meetings are held in which Bobby's teacher, the school counselor, the assistant teacher, and the social worker all go over his progress and strategize ways of helping him become more successful as a student.

Scenario #2: LeShonda

LeShonda is 18 years old and in 11th grade. She repeated a grade in middle school after having an emotional breakdown that forced her to stay at home under a doctor's care for several months. She has been diagnosed with bipolar disorder, and on two occasions in her past she attempted suicide. She is currently taking the antidepressant Zoloft and the bipolar drug lithium under the supervision of a county psychiatrist who sees her once every three months. She is one to two years behind in her academic coursework and receives Cs or Ds in all of her classes except art, where she usually gets As or Bs. Her teachers report that she rarely responds in class, often seems half-asleep (possibly a side effect of her medication), and claims not to know answers when called upon. She often uses negative terms to describe herself (e.g., "I'm too stupid to know the answer"). She has no friends, and she spends lunchtime at a table by herself eating and doodling with a pen on her napkin.

Poor Niche Construction

LaShonda is held back in the 11th grade for her failure to make adequate progress in her coursework. To help her catch up in her studies, her art class has been eliminated and replaced with a remedial math class. Her teachers humorously pick on her in class for being so sleepy. She feels embarrassed when going to the nurse's office every day to pick up her medications, especially since several of her classmates have seen her do this and now whisper to each other that she is "mental" and "might go postal" at any moment. Her psychiatrist has attempted three times to contact the school for a consultation, but administrators have failed to call back—the principal believes that psychiatry is "just a lot of psychobabble" and that psychoactive medications are simply a "crutch."

Positive Niche Construction

A meeting is held with LaShonda and her principal, math teacher, art teacher, mother, psychiatrist (by phone), the school nurse, the school counselor, and the special education teacher to discuss her needs in school. The group decides that LaShonda should take her medications at home, thus avoiding the stigma of going to the nurse's office. Her abilities with art are noted, and the art teacher schedules an art show featuring LaShonda's paintings and drawings along with those of one or two other exceptional art students. The art teacher also suggests several ways in which the math teacher might integrate the arts into her math lessons—for example, by teaching Fibonacci's sequence and fractals. The school counselor teaches LaShonda positive self-talk strategies to use whenever she starts to put herself down. LaShonda joins an after-school art club and begins to socialize during lunchtime with two or three girls who, like herself, are good at drawing. They are working together on a poster for the school's drug prevention program. LaShonda begins reporting to her mother that she really enjoys school, and her grades are starting to improve in all subjects.

Sample Strategies for Applying Positive Niche Construction to Common Core State Standards—12th Grade

Sample Standard: ELA.W.11–12.3b—*Use narrative techniques, such as dialogue, pacing, description, reflection, and multiple plot lines, to develop experiences, events, and/or characters.*

Strength Awareness

Help the student determine what interests or strengths she might use as a topic for her narrative (e.g., if he's interested in racing cars, he might create a narrative that involves a matchup between two world-famous NASCAR champions).

Positive Role Models

- Present the student with information about famous narrative authors who struggled with emotional or behavioral issues (e.g., William Faulkner, Edgar Allan Poe, Charles Dickens, Emily Dickinson, J. K. Rowling), and suggest that he keep a picture of one of them on his desk for inspiration.

- If the student has writer's block, tell him about famous writers who also suffered from this common writer's ailment (e.g., Leo Tolstoy, Ralph Ellison, Virginia Woolf, F. Scott Fitzgerald), and suggest that he think about them whenever he "hits a wall."

Assistive Technologies/Universal Design for Learning

- Use a goal-setting program such as GoalPro to help the student set goals for his narrative writing (e.g., selection of topic[s], number of words in narrative).

- Use a creative-writing software program such as Storybase to guide the student through the process of writing captivating narratives.

Enhanced Human Resources

- Brainstorm in small groups different ideas for narratives and ways to go about writing them with the class.

- Have the student pair up with a typically developing student showing strong character, a mature personality, and empathetic qualities to work on their narratives together.

- Let the student create a collaborative narrative with some of his fellow students.

Strength-Based Learning Strategies

- Have the student create a mind map illustrating all the elements of his narrative.

- If the student has writer's block, provide him with the opportunity to engage in free-writing sessions.
- Suggest that the student keep a writer's journal to work on different aspects of his narrative (e.g., sketches of characters, plot line ideas, sample dialogue).
- Teach the student who says "I can't write" how to replace negative self-talk with positive affirmations (e.g., "I'm an engaging writer").
- Let the student supplement the narrative using art, music, or some other creative approach.

Affirmative Career Aspirations

Suggest to the student that he incorporate his own career aspirations into the narrative in some way (e.g., if he wants to be a musician, suggest that he write a story about a musical virtuoso).

Environmental Modifications

Tell the student about the different ways in which famous writers worked (e.g., Thomas Wolfe wrote standing up, Truman Capote wrote lying down, Jack London put his ideas on slips of paper and ran them along clothing lines). Help him discover comfortable writing habits that are compatible with the rules and resources of the school.

Assessing the Standard

The student shall write a narrative using techniques such as dialogue, pacing, description, reflection, and multiple plot lines to develop experiences, events, or characters. The student may complete the assignment in a writing journal, provide pictures or cartoons to go along with the narrative, or supplement the written narrative with a musical, dramatic, or artistic narrative.

Conclusion

The inclusion of students with emotional and behavioral disorders in the regular classroom is a controversial topic, with some educators arguing for separate classes (Kauffman, Lloyd, Baker, & Riedel, 1995) and others arguing for full inclusion (Lipsky & Gartner, 1997). I believe that this is a false distinction. The question is not whether students with emotional and behavioral disorders should be in a regular classroom or a separate special education classroom, but rather what kind of positive niche we might construct so that the students' strengths are accentuated and the weaknesses minimized. By keeping an open mind, and by having a broad range of options and strategies available, we can really begin to help students who struggle with emotional and behavioral disorders get on the right path to academic achievement in school and optimal growth in life.

For Further Study

1. Select a student with an emotional or behavioral disorder and create a "sociogram" for her—that is, a diagram depicting all of her significant school relationships, including teachers, peers, and support personnel. Indicate negative connections with wiggly lines and positive connections with straight lines. To what extent does the student have a positive support system in place at the school? How could the student's social network be made stronger? Suggestions might include repairing negative relationships, strengthening positive relationships, and bringing other individuals into the student's support system. If possible, include in the sociogram individuals outside the school (e.g., parents, relatives, mental health professionals).

(Continued on next page)

For Further Study *(Continued)*

2. **Create an expressive arts component in your school where students with emotional and behavioral disorders (and other students with disabilities) can sculpt, paint, dramatize, produce music, or engage in other artistic activities.** Is their behavior or emotional state significantly different when they express themselves artistically? Develop an action research project to measure a specific factor (e.g., absences from school, results of self-esteem inventory, number of suspensions) before and after implementing this expressive arts component. What are the implications of your findings for further development of the expressive arts in your school?

3. **What types of spaces are used in your school to isolate students with emotional or behavioral disorders who are disruptive, abusive, or out of control?** How effective are these spaces in stabilizing the students? Examine other spaces and procedures in school that might be used to transform negative energies into positive behavior. (e.g., an expressive arts area, a positive time-out area, a relaxation area, an area for reflecting and learning about self-control). Experiment with using one or more of these areas and monitor their effects on students' behavior.

4. **Analyze the level of rapport that you have with a student who has an emotional or behavioral disorder.** What specific steps might you take to improve your rapport (e.g., use praise more often, recognize the student's interests and strengths, greet the student at the door at the beginning of class)? Choose one or more of these interventions (or others of your choosing) to implement and then evaluate the results.

5. **What is your own position regarding the inclusion of students with emotional or behavioral disorders in the regular classroom?** Share your ideas with your colleagues. To what extent are your beliefs based on your own past experiences with these students?

7 | The Strength-Based School

Including children with significant disabilities helped remind us of the importance of taking delight in the students' daily efforts and growth. Celebrating accomplishments, both small and large, helped fortify us in our quest for continuous improvements and excellence for all.

—*Bill Henderson, elementary school principal*

A strength-based school that practices positive niche construction with neurodiverse students is essentially one that supports inclusive practices. I had the pleasure of visiting such a school when I was in the Boston area not long ago. The William W. Henderson Inclusion Elementary School (formerly known as the Patrick O'Hearn Elementary School) is a K–5 public school in Dorchester, Massachusetts, serving 230 students. About one-third of the school population consists of students with special needs, who are for the most part fully included in the regular classroom. The school has been a high-performing school in the Boston Public School system, and *Ladies' Home Journal* recently named it one of the "10 Most Amazing Schools" in the United States

(Guernsey & Harmon, 2012). The school's principal for 20 years was Bill Henderson, who in 2009 had the honor of having the school named after him. In 2011, he wrote an inspiring account of his own personal journey in confronting blindness (from *retinitis pigmentosa*) and finding his way through countless daily challenges and successes at the school. That book—*The Blind Advantage: How Going Blind Made Me a Stronger Principal and How Including Children with Disabilities Made Our School Better for Everyone* (Henderson, 2011)—could serve as a primer for educators seeking to make differentiated instruction for neurodiverse students a living reality in their schools.

The day that I visited Henderson Elementary, students were putting on a presentation of the Broadway musical *Annie*. I saw children in wheelchairs, children with autism, children with ADHD, and children with Down syndrome all together on stage with their typically developing peers, and everyone was doing a terrific job of performing. Later in the day, I met Richard, a 10-year-old who read for me a marvelously imaginative and well-developed science fiction story. Only later, as I observed him on the playground making his fingers dance in front of his eyes ("stimming"), did I realize that he was on the autistic spectrum. I saw Rachel, who had both physical and intellectual disabilities, smiling away as she worked industriously on a school project with the help of a paraprofessional. I heard students cheer when one of their peers achieved a significant learning goal. This is how the whole day went—seeing children with disabilities flourishing in both academic and nonacademic ways alongside their typically developing peers.

The Components of Positive Niche Construction at Henderson Elementary School

A look at the seven components of positive niche construction that we've examined throughout this book reveals that the Henderson Inclusion Elementary School has implemented just about all of them.

Strength Awareness

Strength awareness is a priority at Henderson—every child is recognized for his or her positive qualities, whether academic, social, emotional, or creative. Bill Henderson has shared some examples of the positive images school personnel hold about different neuro-diverse students:

- The English teacher who depicts Johnny (who has learning disabilities) as a kid who writes great stories using that special computer program;

- The teacher aide who brags about how terrific Chuck (a boy with cognitive delays) has been combining geometric shapes;

- The music specialist who relates how fantastic Ashley (who has autism) sings during music performances;

- The cafeteria worker who shares how helpful Diana (who has emotional disorders) has been cleaning up in the lunch room period; . . .

- The secretary who comments on how much more clearly Irma (who has speech and language delays) is communicating when she runs an errand to the office;

- Maria (a girl with Down syndrome), who informs everyone that she is a 5th grade superstar because of all the books that she has read. (Henderson, 2006, p. 7)

An important dimension of strength awareness at Henderson has to do with holding high expectations for all the students in the school. Students are challenged to push beyond their comfort level to realize as much of their potential as possible. Henderson writes:

We challenge students with Down syndrome as well as our most academically advanced students to read as much as they can. We challenge our students with cerebral palsy as well as our fastest runners to exercise as much as they can. We challenge our non-verbal students as well as our most polished speakers to communicate as effectively as they can. We challenge our students with autism as well as our "social butterflies" to interact as positively as they can. The goal for every child at our school is to "get smarter, feel smarter, and act smarter." (Henderson, 2003)

The results show. Students at Henderson have scored at a high-performing level on the Massachusetts Comprehensive Assessment System (MCAS) in both English language arts and mathematics assessments, and students who take alternate assessments because of cognitive delays or intellectual disabilities usually receive high marks on their portfolios (Henderson, 2011).

Assistive Technologies/Universal Design for Learning

Bill Henderson notes, "For most O'Hearn students with disabilities, the use of some technology was the only way that they could access the curricula" (Henderson, 2011, p. 55). The school collaborated with several organizations, including the Center for Applied Special Technology (CAST), Kurzweil Educational Systems, Easter Seals, and Intel to incorporate alternative technological approaches into academic subjects. Here are some examples:

- Students with reading disabilities used Kurzweil Readers (translating printed text into speech) and interactive digital books that provided written text, pictures, and synthesized speech so they could more easily access content.

- Students with writing, sensory, or fine-motor disabilities used speech-to-text software, tools for writing in Braille, and adapted keyboards.

- Students used both traditional and adapted calculators in mathematics and web-based interactive mathematics programs such as First in Math.

- While studying the lives of Native Americans in 15th century New England, students used a variety of UDL approaches to find information, including digital books that convert text into audio or Braille. Students were given a variety of UDL ways of expressing what they'd learned, including mastering Native American songs and dances, creating murals and pictures, designing role-play skits, and building dioramas. (Henderson, 2011)

Enhanced Human Resources

Henderson Elementary has a comprehensive system of collaboration that is instrumental in furthering the school's mission to ensure a high level of achievement for all students. Each classroom uses co-teaching (e.g., two teachers—one with certification in regular education, and the other with certification in special education). Each teacher works and interacts with all the students. In addition, paraprofessionals work intensively on a one-to-one basis with students who have particularly challenging physical or cognitive disabilities.

The school also retains, mostly in part-time positions, a physical therapist, an occupational therapist, a speech pathologist, and a range of specialists in the arts (e.g., dance teacher, music specialist, visual artist) who provide one-on-one, small-group, whole-class, and whole-school instruction. For example, the music specialist helps teachers with vocabulary development by regularly inserting vocabulary words into group songs. Even the custodian was integrated into the work of helping students when he agreed to let a student with special needs push his cart with him as part of a reward system for completing classroom assignments.

The school has a range of outside support structures, including the use of Boston Public Schools personnel who provide staff development and technical assistance, student teachers and interns from local colleges and universities, volunteers who come in to read one-on-one with students, and members of a Boston law firm who became pen pals with many of the students.

Finally, the school has an extensive peer-tutoring system. Over 90 percent of students in grades 3 to 5, for example, have volunteered to sacrifice one recess per week to engage in peer tutoring assignments with their younger classmates throughout the school year.

Strength-Based Learning Strategies

Henderson Elementary incorporates a wide range of strength-based learning strategies to help students with a broad spectrum of learning needs. Intensive reading remediation programs and multi-sensory strategies are used with dyslexic students. Students with intellectual disorders work on math skills by interacting directly with money in the school store and cooking in the school's "baking café." The school collaborates with the organization Very Special Arts (VSA) to integrate the arts into the curriculum for individuals with disabilities. The drama teacher helps students creatively depict historical situations and characters from literature. The dance specialist works with students to create innovative dance moves that imitate the movements of different types of animals and helps them to kinesthetically "illustrate" the functioning of the human skeletal system. A student with ADHD was encouraged to embellish her written assignments with her own expertly executed artwork. To help with organizational skills, teachers use graphic organizers, visual charts, color-coded folders, and schedules with words, graphics, or Velcro-backed icons.

Environmental Modifications

At Henderson, ADHD students are given supports such as special seat cushions, stools, and squeezable objects for discharging motor activity while engaged with their schoolwork. Students with poor fine-motor control use special hand grips for writing with pens or pencils, and adaptive keyboards and iPads to help with inputting information. Students with speech and language impairments use augmentative and alternative devices. Those with emotional or behavioral disorders have access to quieter areas of the school to release stress, as well as to valued areas of the school as rewards for positive achievement and behavior.

Positive Role Models and Affirmative Career Aspirations

The most visible role model at Henderson is, of course, Bill Henderson himself, who has modeled how to be a successful and creative individual with a disability. The school has also had speakers with a variety of special needs come and talk about their experiences with cerebral palsy, Down syndrome, learning disabilities, and ADHD. Students particularly enjoyed listening to a poet and an actor who spoke of their difficulties with reading, writing, and focusing while at the same time demonstrating their excellence in their chosen professions. As Bill Henderson notes, "These encounters were liberating for many of our students who for the first time felt comfortable talking more openly about their similar conditions with their nondisabled peers" (Henderson, 2011, personal communication).

The Qualities of a Strength-Based School

Now that we've looked at a specific school that provides a living example of how neurodiversity principles and positive niche construction can be implemented for students with special needs, let's examine key characteristics of a strength-based school. We can begin by articulating what a strength-based school *is not*:

- It is *not* a school where teachers teach the "regular" students in the front of the classroom while a group of "special education" students huddle at the back of the room with a "special education" teacher instructing them in remedial strategies.

- It is *not* a school where the primary activities are teacher lecture and students reading textbooks and completing worksheets.

- It is *not* a school where all the students in a given classroom are working on the same thing, in the same way, at the same time.

- It is *not* a school where teachers have lowered expectations for students with special needs.

- It is *not* a school where the most important goal is increasing standardized test scores.

- It is *not* a school where teachers have taught the same way for years and aren't going to change their approach for anyone.

Now, let's consider what a strength-based school *is*:

A strength-based school includes students with and without disabilities in regular classrooms. In addition to neurotypical students and students with the neurodiverse conditions discussed in this book, classrooms in strength-based schools welcome students with other neurological or sensory-based disorders such as language and communication delays, cerebral palsy, epilepsy, spina bifida, cystic fibrosis, blindness, deafness, multiple sclerosis, muscular dystrophy, stroke, brain injury, and multiple disabilities. A strength-based classroom also includes students who are identified as gifted and talented, creative, or high achieving in other ways.

A strength-based school celebrates and teaches about all types of diversities. Along with neurodiversity, a strength-based school engages students in learning about and celebrating diversities of race, ethnic background, gender, culture, and sexual orientation. Here are some strategies that teachers can use to begin to make acceptance of neurodiversity a living reality for their students:

- Provide a wide range of books, films, and other media about people with special needs (see, for example, the bibliography "Children's and Young Adult Books About Disabilities" at www.uwosh.edu/library/emc/Bibliographies/disabilities .pdf and the list "Movies About People with Disabilities" at www.amazon.com/Movies-about-People-With-Disabilities/ lm/11LFXYLRSRZZJ).

- Involve the parents of students with special needs in classroom planning and teaching.

- Have a Neurodiversity Treasure Hunt where students go around the room and discover the strengths of their classmates (see Figure 7.1). The rules are as follows: (1) Students must find classmates who can do the different tasks that are listed on the Neurodiversity Treasure Hunt sheet. (2) If the classmate does a task satisfactorily, he places his initials next to it. (3) Only one person can be used per task, so 10 people must be found who can do the 10 tasks listed. (Tasks can be made more or less challenging depending upon the specific ability levels of the students, or by changing the content to align with the curriculum.)

- Celebrate special events on the calendar related to neurodiversity (e.g., World Down Syndrome Day on March 21, Autistic Pride Day on June 18).

- Share the information about strengths and abilities contained in this book with other teachers, parents, and neurotypical and neurodiverse students.

A strength-based school makes as its top priority the identification of as many talents, intelligences, abilities, interests, and capacities as possible for each and every student with special needs (and for each and every other student as well). Even before students with special needs walk into a strength-based school, teachers should have an in-depth understanding of their strengths. A student's cumulative file is a good place to start. Highlight anything in the file that is positive, including high grades or test scores, positive teacher comments, indicators of achievements or awards, or any other data that seem to indicate a strength (keeping in mind that, for some kids, "strengths" mean "relative strengths"). Type up all the positive data and keep them available as a reference to share at parent conferences and IEP meetings. Also, collect information about strengths from the

> ### 7.1 Neurodiversity Treasure Hunt
>
> **Find someone who can:**
>
> _____ Draw a picture of a dog
>
> _____ Do a dance step
>
> _____ Sing a favorite song
>
> _____ Make up a story about a buffalo and a moose
>
> _____ Explain how an airplane can fly
>
> _____ Tell a recent dream
>
> _____ Name five different kinds of birds that live nearby
>
> _____ Say what he/she would like to be when he/she grows up
>
> _____ Repeat the names of five classmates
>
> _____ Name three favorite foods

student's previous teachers and from specialists such as art or physical education teachers.

Once the student is a member of the classroom, watch what the student does when she is most passionate about learning, or when she has the opportunity to choose among a variety of learning options. These behaviors can be indicators of learning strengths. Use parent-teacher conferences as an opportunity to gather information about a student's strengths. Ask parents beforehand to bring in 10 photos of their child. Then, use these photos as a starting point for discussion in the meeting. Parents will usually bring in photos of their child doing positive things, which can indicate particular abilities or strengths. Use the 165-item Neurodiversity Strengths Checklist (see Figure 7.2) to gather information about students' strengths.

Finally, ask the students themselves to describe their strengths. If there is a relationship of trust between teachers and students, and the students have at least some insight into their own abilities, then teachers can be assured that they are collecting pertinent information that can be helpful in the strengths assessment process.

7.2 Neurodiversity Strengths Checklist

Personal Strengths

_____ Enjoys working independently

_____ Has a good sense of his/her personal strengths and weaknesses

_____ Learns from past mistakes

_____ Has persistence in carrying out assignments or activities

_____ Is courageous in dealing with adversity and/or the unknown

_____ Keeps a personal diary or journal

_____ Has a good sense of humor

_____ Possesses a sense of responsibility

_____ Has strong opinions about controversial topics

_____ Marches to the beat of a different drummer

_____ Handles stressful events well (e.g., is resilient)

_____ Has good character (e.g., honesty, integrity, fairness)

_____ Has the ability to set realistic goals for him-/herself

_____ Has a sense of confidence or high self-esteem

_____ Has good self-discipline

_____ Has personal ambitions in life

_____ Displays good common sense

_____ Possesses personal vitality, vigor, or energy

Communication Strengths

_____ Explains ideas or concepts well to others

_____ Asks good questions

_____ Is a good storyteller

7.2 Neurodiversity Strengths Checklist (Continued)

Communication Strengths (Continued)

_____ Is a good joke teller

_____ Has good listening skills

_____ Handles verbal feedback well (especially negative feedback)

_____ Has good articulation ability

_____ Is able to effectively use nonverbal cues to communicate with others

_____ Is persuasive in getting someone to do something

_____ Has good assertive skills without being pushy

Social Strengths

_____ Has leadership ability

_____ Has a good sense of empathy for others

_____ Enjoys socializing with others

_____ Is good at helping others

_____ Is kind or affectionate toward others

_____ Has at least one good friend

_____ Prefers working with others

_____ Likes to play board games and/or card games with others

_____ Has skill in refereeing disputes between classmates

_____ Is polite and has good manners

_____ Is able to work out his/her own conflicts with others

_____ Works well in groups

_____ Volunteers his/her time in some worthy cause

_____ Belongs to at least one club or social group (e.g., Scouts)

(Continued on next page)

7.2 Neurodiversity Strengths Checklist *(Continued)*

Social Strengths *(Continued)*

_____ Has a good relationship with at least one family member

_____ Is friendly to others

_____ Is good at sharing with others

_____ Follows class rules

_____ Has a good relationship with at least one teacher in the school

_____ Has good personal hygiene

_____ Trusts others without being taken in

_____ Is liked by his peers

Emotional Strengths

_____ Is emotionally sensitive to perceiving the world around him-/her

_____ Has an optimistic attitude toward life

_____ Can tell how he/she is feeling at any given moment

_____ Can easily pick up on the emotional state of another person

_____ Is able to handle strong internal feelings in a constructive manner

_____ Receives "gut feelings" about things

Cognitive Strengths

_____ Has good organizational skills

_____ Has good study skills

_____ Is able to use cognitive strategies (e.g., self-talk) in solving problems

_____ Is able to pay close attention to details

_____ Has a good short-term or long-term memory

7.2 Neurodiversity Strengths Checklist (*Continued*)

Cognitive Strengths (*Continued*)

_____ Is able to think ahead

_____ Is able to become totally absorbed in an activity

_____ Can easily divide his/her attention between two or more activities (i.e., multitask)

Creative Strengths

_____ Expresses him-/herself dramatically

_____ Has a good imagination

_____ Enjoys doodling, drawing, or painting

_____ Likes to act in plays and skits

_____ Works well with clay or other modeling material

_____ Demonstrates creativity in one or more school assignments

_____ Possesses a love of beautiful things

_____ Has ideas for futuristic or fantastic projects

_____ Comes up with ideas that nobody else has thought of

Literacy Strengths

_____ Enjoys reading books

_____ Has good reading comprehension

_____ Enjoys doing word puzzles or playing word games

_____ Is a good writer in one or more genres (e.g., poetry, stories, reports, letters)

_____ Is a good speller

_____ Has a large vocabulary

_____ Enjoys listening to audio books or to someone telling a story or reading out loud

(*Continued on next page*)

7.2 Neurodiversity Strengths Checklist *(Continued)*

Logical Strengths

_____ Does well in science class

_____ Can estimate things easily

_____ Enjoys working with numbers and/or statistics

_____ Is good at solving math problems

_____ Has a chemistry set or other science kit that he/she works with at home

_____ Has an interest in astronomy, chemistry, physics, or biology

_____ Enjoys logical or number games or puzzles like Rubik's cube or Sudoku

_____ Can easily calculate numbers in his/her head

Visual-Spatial Strengths

_____ Has an aptitude for fixing machines

_____ Likes to create three-dimensional structures with building materials

_____ Is good at doing jigsaw puzzles or other visual puzzles

_____ Is able to read maps well

_____ Reports being able to visualize images clearly

_____ Gets information more easily through pictures than words

_____ Is sensitive to the visual world around him-/her

Physical Strengths

_____ Has a good sense of balance

_____ Learns material best when moving around

_____ Likes to ride his/her bike, skateboard, or other self-powered vehicle

7.2 Neurodiversity Strengths Checklist *(Continued)*

Physical Strengths *(Continued)*

_____ Is good at playing team sports like baseball, soccer, basketball, or football

_____ Is good at playing individual sports like tennis, swimming, gymnastics, or golf

_____ Is in good physical health

_____ Likes to dance

_____ Is physically strong

_____ Is a fast runner or has other athletic abilities

_____ Likes to exercise (e.g., weights, aerobics, jogging, treadmill)

_____ Has good physical endurance

_____ Has good physical flexibility

Dexterity Strengths

_____ Has a hobby building model cars, planes, ships, or other similar projects

_____ Displays good handwriting

_____ Likes to juggle or do magic tricks

_____ Enjoys hand crafts like knitting, crocheting, embroidery, or needlepoint

_____ Likes to make things with his/her hands

_____ Has good tactile ability

_____ Enjoys arts and crafts like origami, collage, or pâpier maché

_____ Enjoys woodworking, carpentry, carving, or metal work

_____ Has good eye-hand coordination

(Continued on next page)

7.2 Neurodiversity Strengths Checklist (*Continued*)

Musical Strengths

_____ Is sensitive to the rhythms of music

_____ Enjoys playing a musical instrument

_____ Knows the music and lyrics of many songs

_____ Has a particular interest in one or more musical genres (e.g., rock, classical, jazz)

_____ Enjoys listening to music

_____ Has a good sense of hearing

_____ Has a good sense of pitch

_____ Has a good singing voice

_____ Makes up his/her own tunes or melodies with or without lyrics

Nature Strengths

_____ Has good rapport with animals

_____ Is good at taking care of plants in the classroom or at home

_____ Is sensitive to weather patterns

_____ Takes care of a pet at home or at school

_____ Is concerned about the welfare of the planet

_____ Likes to go hiking or camping in nature

_____ Enjoys studying nature (e.g., insects, plants, birds, rocks, animals)

_____ Likes to hunt or fish

_____ Has a good sense of direction

High-Tech Strengths

_____ Likes to spend time using a computer, tablet, or smart phone

_____ Has a facility for playing video games

_____ Likes to surf the Internet

7.2 Neurodiversity Strengths Checklist *(Continued)*

High-Tech Strengths *(Continued)*

_____ Knows how to set up audiovisual or computer equipment

_____ Likes to text on the phone

_____ Enjoys social media (e.g., blog, Twitter, Facebook)

_____ Enjoys using a still camera or video camera to record events or express him-/herself

_____ Has several favorite movies or TV shows that he/she likes to talk about

_____ Understands at least one computer language

Spiritual Strengths

_____ Enjoys meditation, yoga, or some other form of contemplation

_____ Asks big life questions (e.g., what is the purpose of life?)

_____ Has a deep sense of wisdom

_____ Participates in religious or other spiritual events

_____ Has a philosophical attitude toward life

_____ Has a strong faith in something higher than him-/herself

Cultural Strengths

_____ Has traveled to other countries

_____ Speaks more than one language

_____ Is tolerant of others who have cultural, ethnic, or racial differences

_____ Has pride in his/her own cultural, ethnic, or racial background

_____ Likes to find out about historical events around the world

_____ Enjoys learning about different cultural traditions

(Continued on next page)

7.2 Neurodiversity Strengths Checklist (Continued)

Other Strengths

_____ Likes collecting things (e.g., stamps, coins, buttons)

_____ Loves to cook

_____ Has a love of learning new things

_____ Is a good test taker

_____ Possesses a good memory for nighttime dreams

_____ Is curious about the world around him-/her

_____ Has a good sense of time

_____ Manages money well

_____ Has good fashion sense in the clothes he/she wears

_____ Has good entrepreneurial skills (e.g., has started own business)

A strength-based school makes gifts, talents, and abilities a key part of a student's Individualized Educational Program (IEP). All too often, IEP meetings are filled with negative references to student performance, including low grades, below-average test scores, poor special education assessments, reports of misbehavior (e.g., fights, tantrums), and stories about low academic performance from the student's teachers. It is imperative that the emphasis right from the start be on the positive attributes of the learner.

Recently, a new method of inquiry has emerged that promises to generate an intrinsically affirmative approach to running IEP meetings: Appreciative Inquiry (AI). Originally developed as an organizational development tool for business, AI is increasingly being applied in school settings. According to its originator, David L. Cooperrider:

> [AI] deliberately seeks to discover people's exceptionality—their unique gifts, strengths, and qualities. It actively

searches and recognizes people for their specialties—their essential contributions and achievements. And it is based on principles of equality of voice—everyone is asked to speak about their vision of the true, the good, and the possible. Appreciative Inquiry builds momentum and success because it believes in people. It really is an invitation to a positive revolution. Its goal is to discover in all human beings the exceptional and the essential. (Cooperrider, 2001, p. 12)

Educator Peter Kozik, who has applied Appreciative Inquiry to school-related issues, observes that AI "elicits narratives of success that then create the lens through which the future can be planned" (Kozik, 2008, p. iv). In one study, Kozik analyzed the effect of an AI-IEP Protocol (see Figure 7.3) on IEP meetings. He discovered that use of the protocol increased student turn taking, self-advocacy, and positive, informational, and observational remarks while decreasing negative remarks by participants in the meetings.

Once the IEP meeting is concluded, attention needs to be focused on incorporating the student's strengths directly into the IEP itself. Section 1414(d)(3)(A)(i) of the Individuals with Disabilities Education Improvement Act (IDEIA) requires that students' IEPs include information about strengths. All too often, however, this information amounts to a few vague statements that don't really give a very good picture of a student's abilities (e.g., "good worker," "tries to please," "perseveres"). In addition, the strengths section of IEPs is too often isolated from the other sections and fails to be integrated into a student's learning and behavioral objectives. The Neurodiversity Strengths Checklist in Figure 7.2 provides a means of identifying a broad range of tangible strengths that can be incorporated into a student's IEP goals.

Figure 7.4 offers an example that describes and integrates a student's strengths into an IEP goal related to a Common Core State Standard.

7.3 AI-IEP Protocol: Questions for Discussion at IEP meetings

FIRST, SUCCESS

1) *To the student:* Tell us about some of your successes this year. (If appropriate, add: What have you done well and what has worked well for you? What's been happening to make you successful?)

2) *To the parent:* What successes have you seen your child enjoy this year? (If appropriate, add: tell us about what's been happening to help make your child successful?)

3) *To the teachers and specialists:* What successes have you seen for [the student]? (If appropriate, add: Tell us about what's been happening to help make him/her successful?)

4) *To the group:* What suggestions or changes can you think of to make [the student]'s program work even better?

SECOND, GOALS

5) *To the student:*
- What do you think you'd most love to do when you grow up? (Or: What is your goal in life [or after school]?)
   And
- What do you think you'll need to do to get to do what you love most [or to get to your goal]?
   And
- What have you done so far to get to do what you love most [to move toward your goal]?

6) *To the group:* What kinds of support and help can you provide to make [the student]'s program work toward the goals he/she's set for him/herself?

Source: Peter L. Kozik, "Examining the Effects of Appreciative Inquiry on IEP Meetings and Transition Planning," doctoral dissertation, Syracuse University, June 2008. Used with permission of author.

7.4 Sample IEP Goal

Student: Lenny—14 years old—learning disabilities (dyslexia)

Strengths: Lenny is an active learner who possesses good visual-spatial skills and a strong, kinesthetic style of learning. He's scored above average on the block design subtest of WISC-R, achieved high grades in physical education and shop class, and enjoys athletics (baseball, hockey) and making things with his hands (he recently built an inlaid chess table and a cribbage board). In language arts, Lenny enjoys and has a facility for making up stories using Dragon Naturally Speaking. He is popular with his peers and regularly pals around with three or four buddies. He's able to work independently quite well and has enjoyed creating a project this year based on the lives of his favorite sports heroes. He has a bit of the performer in him and enjoys doing magic tricks to entertain the class. At home he cares for his golden retriever and has a small area in the garage where he likes to tinker around with old machines that he's found in secondhand stores.

Common Core State Standard Goal: ELA.9–10.RI.7—Analyze various accounts of a subject told in different mediums (e.g., a person's life story in both print and multimedia), determining which details are emphasized in each account.

Plan: Lenny will read a biography of his hero Alex Rodriguez using a Kurzweil Reader and watch a documentary based on his life. He will then map out at least five key details for each account on a graphic organizer (using Kidspiration) and present an oral report to the class analyzing the details in each account, followed by a performance of some of his best magic tricks.

Conclusion

Now that we've explored several qualities of the strength-based school, let's return to Mr. Farmington's 5th grade classroom, which we introduced in Chapter 1, and see how his school year with the six special education students and 24 regular education students is shaping up.

It's Week 10 in Mr. Farmington's 5th grade class, and the students are doing a unit on the Civil War.

Stuart, who has autism and loves studying military battles, has become the classroom expert on Civil War battles, explaining some of its key conflicts using miniature soldiers from his own personal collection.

Robert, who has learning disabilities and is "machine-smart," is preparing a report on how different Civil War–era weapons such as the muzzle-loading cannon and the breech-loading Burnside carbine worked mechanically. He is making meticulous drawings of these weapons.

Audrey, who has Down syndrome and loves to partner with other students, has buddied up with Sylvia, one of the best readers in the class. They are taking turns reading books to each other on the Civil War (Audrey is reading the picture book Cecil's Story, *and Sylvia is reading* Soldier's Heart).

Zeke, who has an emotional disorder and is an artist, is painting a series of pictures of famous Civil War battles, including Gettysburg, Shiloh, and Chickamauga, and plans to talk about these battles using his paintings as a reference point.

Guy, who has ADHD and loves drama, is part of a group of students in the class who are preparing a mock trial of a Confederate soldier (played by Guy) who is accused of treason against the United States.

In Mr. Farmington's classroom, every student is busily engaged in exploring a different aspect of the Civil War—some on their own, others with help from classmates. It would be wrong to say that Mr. Farmington has "accommodated" to his students' disabilities. The kids are fully engaged in a learning process that, above all, makes use of their talents, interests, and abilities. At the same time, they're given the opportunity to work through their difficulties. Stuart must break out of his social isolation in order to share his hobby with the class. Robert needs to accompany his drawings with written explanations and will receive help from Billy, one of the best writers in the class. Sylvia is helping Audrey with her language arts skills as they read together.

Interestingly, the human resources that matter the most in Mr. Farmington's class are peer relationships, and the strength-based learning strategies that seem to work best here are those that rely on project-based learning. In a classroom focused on lectures, textbooks, and worksheets, there would be far fewer opportunities for Mr. Farmington's neurodiverse students to shine. When we embrace a strength-based paradigm grounded in differentiated instruction and positive niche construction, however, we embark upon a path that uses the widest range of student-centered interventions and builds upon each student's core capacity of strengths.

A strength-based classroom is not a "regular classroom" that includes students with disabilities. This conceptualization carries with it the idea that there is a "normal classroom" to which modifications will need to be made in order to meet the learning needs of a minority of students with disabilities. In this traditional model, students with disabilities are "guests" in somebody else's house and ought to be grateful for the chance to "learn with normal students." This sort of arrangement has a condescending quality to it. Teachers might think, "I'd prefer not have these kids in my class, but since I'm required to by law, I have no other option than to provide for their needs." A strength-based classroom is a place where students with all sorts of labels come together as equals to form a new type of learning environment: one where there is no such thing as a normal student, and where each and every learner is viewed as a marvel.

For Further Study

1. Read a book on the topic of inclusion. Possibilities include *The Blind Advantage,* by Bill Henderson (noted earlier in this chapter); *Brain-Friendly Strategies for the Inclusion Classroom,* by Judy Willis; *Creating an Inclusive School,* 2nd edition, edited by Richard Villa and Jacqueline Thousand; *Inclusive Schools in Action,* by James McLeskey and Nancy Waldron; or any book published by Inclusion Press (www.inclusion.com/inclusionpress.html). How do inclusive practices fit in with the components of positive niche construction? How might an approach based on strengths serve as a means for implementing inclusion in the schools?

2. Use the AI-IEP Protocol (Figure 7.3) to conduct a student's IEP meeting. Pay attention to which of the seven components of positive niche construction have already been incorporated into the student's IEP, and discuss what additional improvements might be made to the student's plan based upon strengths, interests, and goals for the future.

3. Examine the "strengths" section of a student's IEP. How do the strengths listed convey an accurate view of the student's abilities? How might this section be improved upon? Use the Neurodiversity Strengths Checklist (Figure 7.2) to expand the number of strengths reported in the student's IEP. Are the student's strengths incorporated into the rest of the IEP? How might these strengths be better integrated into the student's learning goals?

4. **Locate a school in your area that practices schoolwide inclusion. Contact the administrator and plan a school visit.** Notice how many of the components of positive niche construction are used to help facilitate their inclusive practices. What is the overall climate of the school in terms of honoring a wide diversity of learners? What elements can you take away from this school to apply in your own school setting?

5. **Engage in an action research project inquiring into the effectiveness of identifying and developing neurodiverse students' strengths as a way of helping them to become more successful learners.** Use the Neurodiversity Strengths Checklist (Figure 7.2) as an informal instrument to find out more about the strengths of one or more of your neurodiverse students. Then use your knowledge of those strengths to develop more affirmative interventions to help them succeed.

6. **Create a display in a prominent area of your school titled "Celebrating Strengths in All Our Learners!"** In this display, include samples of school work and photos of kids with special needs learning alongside typically developing students, where everyone is engaged in active learning projects, assignments, and programs. Alternatively, put on a "Celebrating Neurodiversity Week" during which the strengths of neurodiverse and neurotypical students are showcased (e.g., musical performances, storytelling, dramatic performances, project presentations, athletic events, science fair projects, poetry slams, and more).

References

Andrade, J. (2010). What does doodling do? *Applied Cognitive Psychology*, *24*(1), 100–106.

Andrews, L. W. (2005, Fall). Employees with intellectual disabilities find new job niches. *Managing Smart.*

Antonetta, S. (2007). *A mind apart: Travels in a neurodiverse world.* New York: Tarcher.

Appleyard, D. (1997, February 27). Education: The art of being dyslexic. *The Independent.* Retrieved from http://www.independent.co.uk/news/education/education-news/education-the-art-of-being-dyslexic-1280776.html

Armstrong, T. (1988). Describing strengths in children labeled "learning disabled" using Howard Gardner's theory of multiple intelligences as an organizing framework. *Dissertation Abstracts International, 48*(8A), 2038–2039.

Armstrong, T. (1996, May/June). Labels can last a lifetime. *Learning, 24*(6), 41–42.

Armstrong, T. (1997). *The myth of the A.D.D. child: 50 ways to improve your child's behavior and attention without drugs, labels, or coercion.* New York: Plume.

Armstrong, T. (1999). *7 kinds of smart: Identifying and developing your multiple intelligences.* New York: Plume.

Armstrong, T. (2000). *In their own way: Discovering and encouraging your child's multiple intelligences.* New York: Tarcher/Penguin.

Armstrong, T. (2001, November). IKSWAL: Interesting kids saddled with alienating labels. *Educational Leadership. 59*(3), 38–41.

Armstrong, T. (2009). *Multiple intelligences in the classroom* (3rd ed.). Alexandria, VA: ASCD.

Armstrong, T. (2011). *The power of neurodiversity: Unleashing the advantages of your differently wired brain.* Cambridge, MA: DeCapo/Perseus.

Austin, R., Wareham, J., & Busquets, X. (2008). *Specialisterne: Sense & details.* Cambridge, MA: Harvard Business Publishing.

Autism and the concept of neurodiversity [special issue]. (2010). *Disability Studies Quarterly, 30*(1). Retrieved from http://dsq-sds.org/issue/view/43

Baker, D. L. (2010). *The politics of neurodiversity: Why public policy matters.* Boulder, CO: Lynne Rienner Publishers.

Bandura, A. (1986). *Social foundations of thought and action: A social-cognitive theory.* Englewood Cliffs, NJ: Prentice Hall.

Baron-Cohen, S. (1998). Superiority on the embedded figures task in autism and in normal males: Evidence of an "innate talent"? *Behavioral and Brain Sciences, 21*(3), 408–409.

Baron-Cohen, S. (2002). Is Asperger's syndrome necessarily viewed as a disorder? *Focus on Autism and Other Developmental Disabilities, 17*(3), 186–191.

Baron-Cohen, S. (2003). *The essential difference: The truth about the male and female brain.* New York: Basic Books.

Bennett, D. E., Zentall, S. S., French, B. F., & Giorgetti-Borucki, K. (2006, February). The effects of computer-administered choice on students with and without characteristics of attention deficit/hyperactivity disorder. *Behavioral Disorders, 31*(2), 189–203.

Benson, P. L. (1997). *All kids are our kids: What communities must do to raise caring and responsible children and adolescents.* New York: Jossey-Bass.

Biesta, G. (2007). Why "what works" won't work: Evidence-based practice and the democratic deficit in educational research. *Educational Theory, 57*(1), 1–22.

Blood, E., Johnson, J. W., Ridenour, L., Simmons, K., & Crouch, S. (2011, August). Using an iPod touch to teach social and self-management skills to an elementary student with emotional/behavioral disorders. *Education and Treatment of Children, 34*(3), 299–321.

Blume, H. (1998, September 30). Neurodiversity. *Atlantic.* Retrieved from http://www.theatlantic.com/magazine/archive/1998/09/neurodiversity/5909/

Bohmann, R. R. (2003). *Class meetings as a tool for classroom management and character development: An annotated bibliography.* (ERIC Document Reproduction Service No. ED 478 005)

Borthwick, C. (1996). Racism, I.Q., and Down syndrome. *Disability & Society, 11*(3), 403–410.

Bowman-Perrott, L. (2009, May). Classwide peer tutoring: An effective strategy for students with emotional and behavioral disorders. *Intervention in School & Clinic, 44*(5), 259–267.

Branson, R. (1998). *Losing my virginity: How I've survived, had fun, and made a fortune doing business my way.* New York: Times Business.

Broer, S. M., Doyle, M. B., & Giangreco, M. F. (2005, Summer). Perspectives of students with intellectual disabilities about their experiences with paraprofessional support. *Exceptional Children, 71*(4), 415–430.

Brooks, D. (2007, September 14). The waning of I.Q. *New York Times.* Retrieved from http://www.nytimes.com/2007/09/14/opinion/14brooks.html?_r=3

Brooks, R., & Goldstein, S. (2001). *Raising resilient children.* New York: Contemporary Books.

Burke, C., & McDaniel, J. B. (1991). *A special kind of hero.* New York: Doubleday.

Buzan, T. (1996). *The mind map book: How to use radiant thinking to maximize your brain's untapped potential.* New York: Plume.

Byrne, D. L. (2008). *The effects of participative goal setting on Aggression Replacement Training for middle school students with emotional and behavioral disorders.* Ann Arbor, MI: ProQuest.

Calavita, K. (2010). *Invitation to law & society: An introduction to the study of real law.* Chicago: University of Chicago Press.

Capacchione, L. (2008). *The creative journal for teens: Making friends with yourself.* Pompton Plains, NJ: Career Press.

Carey, B. (2006, February 14). West Wing blues: It's lonely at the top. *New York Times.* Retrieved from http://www.nytimes.com/2006/02/14/science/14find.html

Carter, E. W., Lane, K. L., Pierson, M. R., & Glaeser, B. (2006, Spring). Self-determination skills and opportunities of transition-age youth with emotional disturbance and learning disabilities. *Exceptional Children, 72*(3), 333–346.

Cartwright, S. (1851). Diseases and peculiarities of the Negro race. *De Bow's Review.* Retrieved from http://www.pbs.org/wgbh/aia/part4/4h3106t.html

CAST Inc. (1999–2012). What is universal design for learning? Retrieved from http://www.cast.org/udl/index.html

Center for Applied Special Technology. (2012). *UDL and Common Core FAQs.* Retrieved from http://www.udlcenter.org/advocacy/faq_guides/common_core

Centers for Disease Control and Prevention. (2010, November 12). Increased prevalence of parent-reported attention deficit/hyperactivity disorder children—United States, 2003 and 2007. *Morbidity and Mortality Weekly Report, 59*(44), 1439–1443.

Centers for Disease Control and Prevention. (2012, March 20). Prevalence of autism spectrum disorders—autism and developmental disabilities monitoring network, 14 sites, United States, 2008. *Morbidity and Mortality Weekly Report, 61*(SS03), 1–19.

Cherniss, C. (2006). *School change and the MicroSociety program.* Thousand Oaks, CA: Corwin Press.

Children's Hospital Boston. (2005–2011). *Fragile X syndrome program at Children's Hospital Boston.* Retrieved from http://www.childrenshospital.org/clinicalservices/Site2242/mainpageS2242P0.html

Clark, R. W. (2001). *Einstein: The life and times.* New York: Avon.

Clegg, S. (2005, July). Evidence-based practice in educational research: A critical realist critique of systematic review. *British Journal of Sociology of Education, 26*(3), 415–428.

Clement, R. (1994). *Counting on Frank.* Boston: Houghton Mifflin School.

Cohen, H. C., & Bailer, B. (1999, August 1). Lazy, crazy, or stupid. *Fire Chief.* Retrieved from http://firechief.com/mag/firefighting_lazy_crazy_stupid

Colangelo, N., Assouline, S. G., Kerr, B., Huesman, R., & Johnson, D. (1993). Mechanical inventiveness: A three phase study. In G. Bock & K. Ackrill (Eds.), *The origins and development of high ability* (pp. 160–174). New York: Wiley.

Common Core State Standards Initiative. (2011). *Application to students with disabilities.* Retrieved from http://www.corestandards.org/assets/application-to-students-with-disabilities.pdf

Cooperrider, D. L. (2001) Why appreciative inquiry? In C. Royal & S. A. Hammond (Eds.), *Lessons from the field: Applying appreciative inquiry.* Bend, OR: Thin Book Publishing.

Cornwell, J. (2007, July 1). Master of creation? Retrieved from http://www.martinfrost.ws/htmlfiles/july2007/master_creation.html.

Cramond, B. (1994). Attention-deficit hyperactivity disorder and creativity: What is the connection? *Journal of Creative Behavior, 38*(3), 193–210.

Cramond, B. (1995). *The coincidence of attention deficit hyperactivity disorder and creativity.* Storrs: The National Research Center on the Gifted and Talented, University of Connecticut.

Cumming, T. M. (2010, March). Using technology to create motivating social skills lessons. *Intervention in School and Clinic, 45*(4), 242–250.

112th Cong. (2011). The current state of employment of persons with intellectual and developmental disabilities, (Testimony of Sharon Lewis). Retrieved from http://www.hhs.gov/asl/testify/2011/03/t20110302a.html

Danforth, S., & Morris, P. (2006, March/May). Orthodoxy, heresy, and the inclusion of American students considered to have emotional/behavioural disorders. *International Journal of Inclusive Education, 10*(2/3), 135–148.

Dautenhahn, K., Nehaniv, C. L., Walters, M. L., Robins, B., Kose-Bagci, H., Mirza, N. A., & Blow, M. (2009). *KASPAR: A minimally expressive humanoid robot for human-robot interaction.* Hartfield, United Kingdom: University of Hertfordshire. Retrieved from http://oxfordbrookes.academia.edu/MikeBlow/Papers/236930/KASPAR_a_Minimally_Expressive_Humanoid_Robot_for_Human_robot_Interaction_Research

Davison, P. (2011, July 1). Study: Video games can help young people with learning difficulties. Retrieved from Chris Jones Gaming at http://www.chrisjonesgaming.net/study-video-games-can-help-young-people-with-learning-difficulties/

Dawson, M., Soulières, I., Gernsbacher, M. A., & Mottron, L. (2007, August). The level and nature of autistic intelligence. *Psychological Science, 8*(8), 657–662.

Double-tongued dictionary. (2004). Neurodiversity. Retrieved from http://www.doubletongued.org/index.php/dictionary/neurodiversity/

Down, J. L. (1866). Observations on an ethnic classification of idiots. *London Hospital Reports, 3,* 259–262. Retrieved from http://www.neonatology.org/classics/down.html

Dunn, R. & Dunn, K. (1992). *Teaching elementary students through their individual learning style.* Boston: Allyn & Bacon.

DuPaul, G. J., Erven, R. A., Hook, C. L., & McGoey, K .E. (1998). Peer tutoring for children with attention deficit hyperactivity disorder: Effects on classroom behavior and academic performance. *Journal of Applied Behavioral Analysis, 31*(4), 579–592.

Dwight, V. (2010, February). All eyes on iPad. Retrieved from Great Schools at http://www.greatschools.org/special-education/other-disorders/2073-iPad-essay.gs

Dykens, E. M. (2006). Toward a positive psychology of mental retardation. *American Journal of Orthopsychiatry, 76*(2), 185–193.

Edelman, G. (1987). *Neural Darwinism: The theory of neuronal group selection.* New York: Basic Books.

Edelman, G. (1998, Spring). Building a picture of the brain. *Daedalus, 127*(2), 37–69.

Fisher, S. (2008, April 5). Appreciative inquiry and strengths in the special education process. *Positive Psychology News Daily.* Retrieved from http://positivepsychologynews.com/news/sherri-fisher/20080405702

Fitzpatrick, M., & Knowlton E. (2009, Summer). Bringing evidence-based self-directed intervention practices to the trenches for students with emotional and behavioral disorders. *Preventing School Failure, 53*(4), 253–266.

Forster, E. S. (1927). *The works of Aristotle, Vol. VII: Problemata XXX*. Oxford: Clarendon Press. Retrieved from http://archive.org/stream/worksofaris totle07arisuoft/worksofaristotle07arisuoft_djvu.txt

Foxx, R. M. (2008, October). Applied behavior analysis treatment of autism: The state of the art. *Child and Adolescent Psychiatric Clinics of North America, 17*(4), 821–834.

Frith, U. (Ed. and Trans.). (1991). *Autism and Asperger syndrome*. Cambridge: Cambridge University Press.

Gallup Youth Development Specialists. (2007). *StrengthsExplorer for Ages 10 to 14* (2nd ed.). Washington, DC: Gallup Press.

Gardner, H. (1993). *Frames of mind: The theory of multiple intelligences*. New York: Basic Books.

Geschwind, N. (1982). Why Orton was right. *Annals of Dyslexia, 32*(1), 13–30.

Gevensleben, H., Holl, B., Albrecht, B., Vogel, C., Schlamp, D., Kratz, O., Studer, P., Rothenberger, A., Moll, G. H., & Heinrich, H. (2009, June). Is neurofeedback an efficacious treatment for ADHD? A randomized controlled clinical trial. *Journal of Child Psychology and Psychiatry, 50*(7), 780–789.

Gillham, J. E., with Reivich, K. J., Freres, D. R., Lascher, M., Litzinger, S., Shatté, A., & Seligman, M. E. P. (2006, Fall). School-based prevention of depression and anxiety symptoms in early adolescence: A pilot of a parent intervention component. *School Psychology Quarterly, 21*(3), 323–348.

Goldbeck, L., & Schmid, K. (2003, September). Effectiveness of autogenic relaxation training on children and adolescents with behavioral and emotional problems. *Journal of the American Academy of Child & Adolescent Psychiatry, 42*(9), 1046–1054.

Gould, S. J. (1977). *Ontogeny and phylogeny*. Cambridge, MA: Harvard University Press.

Grandin, T. (1996). *Thinking in pictures: And other reports from my life with autism*. New York: Vintage.

Grandin, T. (2004). *Developing talents: Careers for individuals with Asperger syndrome and high-functioning autism*. Overland Park, KS: Autism Asperger Publishing Company.

Grandin, T. (2005). *Animals in translation: Using the mysteries of autism to decode animal behavior*. New York: Harcourt.

Greenspan, S., & Wieder, S. (2009). *Engaging autism: Using the Floortime approach to help children relate, communicate, and think*. Cambridge, MA: DaCapo/Perseus.

Guernsey, L., & Harmon, S. (2012). America's most amazing schools. *Ladies Home Journal*. Retrieved from http://www.lhj.com/relationships/family/school/most-amazing-schools/?page=2

Gulchak, D. J. (2008). Using a mobile handheld computer to teach a student with an emotional and behavioral disorder to self-monitor attention. *Education and Treatment of Children, 31*(4), 567–581.

Hartmann, T. (1997). *Attention deficit disorder: A different perception.* Nevada City, CA: Underwood Books.

Heathfield, L. T., & Clark, E. (2004). Shifting from categories to services: Comprehensive school-based mental health for children with emotional disturbance and social maladjustment. *Psychology in the Schools, 41*(8), 911–920.

Henderson, W. (2003, Spring). High expectations and developmental disabilities. *Developmental Disabilities Leadership Forum, 3*(1).

Henderson, B. (2006). Champions of inclusion: Making the extraordinary ordinary. *International Journal of Whole Schooling, 3*(1), 7–12.

Henderson, B. (2011). *The blind advantage: How going blind made me a stronger principal and how including children with disabilities made our school better for everyone.* Cambridge, MA: Harvard Education Press.

Hendrickx, S. (2010). *The adolescent and adult neuro-diversity handbook: Asperger's syndrome, ADHD, dyslexia, dyspraxia, and related conditions.* London: Jessica Kingsley Publishers.

Hewitt, M. B. (2005). Meeting the challenge of inclusion for students with emotional disabilities. Retrieved from Spark Action at http://sparkaction.org/node/29849

Hipsky, S. (2007, Summer). Drama discovery: Setting the stage for students with emotional/behavioral needs to learn about Self. *Essays in Education, 21,* 163–182.

Howell, W., West, M., & Peterson, P. E. (2008, Fall). The 2008 Education Next PEPG survey of public opinion. *Education Next, 8*(4). Retrieved from http://educationnext.org/the-2008-education-nextpepg-survey-of-public-opinion/

Hutchings, B. L., & Olsen, R. V. (2008). *A school for everyone: School design to support the inclusion of students with disabilities.* Newark: Center for Architecture and Building Science Research, New Jersey Institute of Technology.

Individuals with Disabilities Education Improvement Act of 2004, 20 U.S.C. § 1400 *et seq.*

Jamison, K. R. (1996). *Touched with fire: Manic-depressive illness and the artistic temperament.* New York: Free Press.

Jensen, P. S., Mrazek, D., Knapp, P. K., Steinberg, L., Pfeffer, C., Schowalter, J., & Shapiro, T. (1997, December). Evolution and revolution in child psychiatry: ADHD as a disorder of adaptation. *Journal of the American Academy of Child and Adolescent Psychiatry, 36*(12), 1672–1679.

Jolivette, K., Stichter, J. P., Nelson, C. M., Scott, T. M., & Liaupsin, C. J. (2000, August). Improving post-school outcomes for students with emotional and behavior disorders. Retrieved from Council for Exceptional Children at http://www.cec.sped.org/AM/Template.cfm?Section=Search&template=/CM/HTMLDisplay.cfm&ContentID=1856

Kalis, T. M., Vannest, K. J., & Parker, R. (2007, Spring). Praise counts: Using self-monitoring to increase effective teaching practices. *Preventing School Failure, 51*(3), 20–27.

Karolyi, C. V., Winner, E., Gray, W., & Sherman, G. (2003, June). Dyslexia linked to talent: Global visual-spatial ability. *Brain and Language, 85*(3), 427–431.

Kauffman, J. M., Lloyd, J. W., Baker, J., & Riedel, T. M. (1995). Inclusion of all students with emotional or behavioral disorders? Let's think again. *Phi Delta Kappan, 76*(7), 542–546.

Kessler, R. C., Chiu, W. T., Demler, O., Merikangas, K. R., & Walters, E. E. (2005). Prevalence, severity, and comorbidity of twelve-month DSM-IV disorders in the national comorbidity survey replication (NCS-R). *Archives of General Psychiatry, 62*(6), 617–627.

Kingsley, J., & Levitz, M. (1994). *Count us in: Growing up with Down syndrome.* New York: Harcourt.

Kohn, A. (1999). *Punished by rewards: The trouble with gold stars, incentive plans, As, praise, and other bribes.* Boston: Mariner Books.

Kozik, P. L. (2008, June). *Examining the effects of appreciative inquiry on IEP meetings and transition planning* (doctoral dissertation). Retrieved from http://appreciativeinquiry.case.edu/uploads/PL%20Kozik%20Dissertation%208-08.pdf

Kramer, P. D. (2005, April 17). There's nothing deep about depression. *New York Times Magazine.* Retrieved from http://www.nytimes.com/20/04/17/magazine/17DEPRESSION.html

Krane, B. (2010, July 14). CHIP research: Robots may help children with autism. *CHIP Today.* Retrieved from http://www.chip.uconn.edu/2010/07/chip-researchers-robots-may-help-children-with-autism/

Kuo, F. E., & Taylor, A. F. (2004, September). A potential natural treatment for attention deficit/hyperactivity disorder. *American Journal of Public Health, 94*(9), 1580–1586.

Law, S., & Scott, S. (1995, June). Tips for practitioners: Pet care: A vehicle for learning. *Focus on Autistic Behavior, 10*(2), 17–18.

Lenhoff, H., Perales, O., & Hickok, G. (2001). Absolute pitch in Williams syndrome. *Musical Perception, 18*(3), 491–503.

Lenhoff, H. M., Wang, P. P., Greenberg, F., & Bellugi, U. (1997, December). Williams syndrome and the brain. *Scientific American, 277*(6), 68–73.

Levitin, D. J., Cole, K., Chiles, M., Lai, Z., Lincoln, A., & Bellugi, U. (2004). Characterizing the musical phenotype in individuals with Williams syndrome. *Neuropsychology, Development, and Cognition, Section C, Child Neuropsychology, 10*(4), 223–247.

Lewin, K. (1997). *Resolving social conflicts and field theory in social science.* Washington, DC: American Psychological Association.

Lewis, T. J., Jones, S. E. L., Horner, R. H., & Sugai, G. (2010). School-wide positive behavior support with emotional/behavioral disorders: Implications for prevention, identification, and intervention. *Exceptionality, 18*(2), 82–93.

Lewontin, R. C. (2010, May 27). Not so natural selection. *New York Review of Books, 57*(9). Retrieved from http://www.nybooks.com/articles/archives/2010/may/27/not-so-natural-selection/

Life Skills. (2009, October 15). *Benefits of employing people with disabilities.* Retrieved from http://www.disabled-world.com/disability/employment/usa/benefits-employing-disabilities.php

Lipsky, D. K., & Gartner, A. (1997). *Inclusion and school reform: Transforming America's classrooms.* Baltimore: Brookes.

Lopata, C., Nida, R. E., & Marable, M. A. (2006, March/April). Progressive muscle relaxation: Preventing aggression in students with EBD. *Teaching Exceptional Children, 8*(4), 20–25.

Ludwig, A. (1995). *The price of greatness: Resolving the creativity and madness controversy.* New York: Guilford Press.

Malbin, D. (2002). *Fetal alcohol spectrum disorders: Trying differently rather than harder.* Portland, OR: FASCETS.

Mallet, K. (2011, November 14). *Skilled readers rely on their brains' "visual dictionary" to recognize words* [Press release]. Georgetown University Medical Center. Retrieved from http://explore.georgetown.edu/news/?ID=60788&PageTemplateID=295

McDuffie, K. A., Landrum, T. J., & Gelman, J. A. (2008, Winter). Co-teaching and students with emotional and behavioral disorders. *Beyond Behavior, 17*(2), 11–16.

Michalko, M. (2006). *Thinkertoys: A handbook of creative thinking techniques* (2nd ed.). Berkeley, CA: Ten Speed Press.

Montagu, A. (1988). *Growing young* (2nd ed.). Westport, CT: Bergin & Garvey.

Morris, B. (2002, May 13). Overcoming dyslexia. *Fortune.* Retrieved from http://money.cnn.com/magazines/fortune/fortune_archive/2002/05/13/322876/index.htm

Moses, S. (1990, February). Hypotheses on ADHD debated at conference. *APA Monitor, 23*(2), 34.

Mottron, L. (2011, November 2). The power of autism. *Nature, 479,* 33–35.

Mottron, L., Dawson, M., Soulières, I., Hubert, B., & Burack, J. (2006, January). Enhanced perceptual functioning in autism: An update and eight principles of autistic perception. *Journal of Autism and Developmental Disorders, 36*(1), 27–43.

Mundi, P., Sigman, M., Kasari, C., & Yirmiya, N. (1988, February). Nonverbal communication skills in Down syndrome children. *Child Development, 59*(1), 235–249.

Myers, I. B. (1995). *Gifts differing: Understanding personality type*. Boston: Nicholas Brealey Publishing.

National Disability Rights Network. (2010, January). *Segregated and exploited: The failure of the disability service system to provide quality work*. Retrieved from http://www.hdi.uky.edu/setp/Materials/Segregated-and-Exploited_v18.pdf

Nauert, R. (2010, January 11). Biofeedback helps kids with ADHD. Retrieved from PsychCentral at http://psychcentral.com/news/2010/01/11/biofeedback-helps-kids-with-adhd/10669.html

Nelsen, J. (1999). *Positive time-out: And over 50 ways to avoid power struggles in the home and the classroom*. Roseville, CA: Prima Publishing.

Niesyn, M. E. (2009). Strategies for success: Evidence-based instructional practices for students with emotional and behavioral disorders. *Preventing School Failure, 53*(4), 227–233.

Norwich, B., & Kelly, N. (2004, February). Pupils' views on inclusion: Moderate learning difficulties and bullying in mainstream and special schools. *British Educational Research Journal, 30*(1), 43–65.

Odling-Smee, F. J., Laland, K. N., & Feldman, M. W. (2003). *Niche construction: The neglected process in evolution*. Princeton, NJ: Princeton University Press.

Osgood, R. L. (2007). *The history of special education: A struggle for equality in American public schools*. Santa Barbara, CA: Praeger.

Overy, K. (2003, November). Dyslexia and music. *Annals of the New York Academy of Sciences, 999*, 497–505.

Pardun, C. J. (2005, February). Media's portrayal of people with intellectual disabilities. Retrieved from Special Olympics at http://www.specialolympics.org/uploadedFiles/LandingPage/WhatWeDo/Research_Studies_Desciption_Pages/Policy_paper_media_portrayal.pdf

Paugh, P., & Dudley-Marling, C. (2011, September). Speaking deficit into (or out of) existence: How language constrains classroom teachers' knowledge about instructing diverse learners. *International Journal of Inclusive Education, 15*(8), 819–833.

Poe, E. A. (1850/2004). *Eleonora*. Charleston, SC: BookSurge Classics.

Pollock, D. (2009). *Neurodiversity in higher education: Positive responses to specific learning differences*. New York: Wiley.

Poplin, M. (1984, Spring). Summary rationalizations, apologies, and farewell: What we don't know about the learning disabled. *Learning Disability Quarterly, 7*(2), 130–134.

Project SEARCH (2011–2012). High school transition program. Retrieved from http://www.projectsearch.us/OurPROGRAM/HighSchoolTransition.aspx

Rahman, S. A., & Rahman, A. (2010). Efficacy of virtual reality-based therapy on balance in children with Down syndrome. *World Applied Sciences Journal, 10*(3), 254–261.

Reddy, V., Williams, E., & Vaughan, A. (2001). Shared laughter: The humour of pre-school children with Down syndrome. *Down Syndrome Research and Practice, 7*(3), 125–128.

Reinhart, M. (2003). *Young naturalists' handbook: Insect-lo-pedia*. New York: Hyperion.

Rizzolatti, G., & Craighero, L. (2004). The mirror-neuron system. *Annual Review of Neuroscience, 27,* 169–192.

Robelen, E. (2012, March 9). Teacher survey highlights cuts to the arts, foreign languages. *Education Week*. Retrieved from http://blogs.edweek.org/edweek/curriculum/2012/03/a_new_teacher_survey_offers.html

Rosal, M. L. (1993). Comparative group art therapy research to evaluate changes in locus of control in behavior disordered children. *The Arts in Psychotherapy, 20*(3), 231–241.

Rose, D., & Meyer, A. (2002). *Teaching every student in the digital age: Universal Design for Learning*. Alexandria, VA: ASCD.

Rose, D. H., Hasselbring, T. S., Stahl, S., & Zabala, J. (2005). Assistive technology and Universal Design for Learning: Two sides of the same coin. In D. Edyburn, K. Higgins, & R. Boone (Eds.), *Handbook of special education technology research and practice* (pp. 507–518). Whitefish Bay, WI: Knowledge by Design.

Rosenthal, R., & Jacobson, L. (2003). *Pygmalion in the classroom: Teacher expectation and pupils' intellectual development*. Williston, VT: Crown House.

Rosenzweig, M., Bennett, E., & Diamond, M. (1972, February). Brain changes in response to experience. *Scientific American, 226*(2), 22–29.

Rudy, L. J. (2009, September 3). Autistic traits: A plus for many careers. Retrieved from About.com at http://autism.about.com/od/transitioncollegejobs/p/autismskills.htm

Sacks, O. (1996). *An anthropologist on Mars: Seven paradoxical tales*. New York: Vintage.

Sacks, O. (1998). *The man who mistook his wife for a hat and other clinical tales*. New York: Touchstone.

Sacks, O. (2008). *Musicophilia: Tales of music and the brain*. New York: Vintage.

Salmon, H. (2006, January). Educating students with emotional or behavioral disorders. *Law and Disorder, 1*, 9–53.

Schilling, D. L., Washington, K., Billingsley, F. F., & Deitz, J. (2003, September/October). Classroom seating for children with attention deficit hyperactivity disorder: Therapy balls versus chairs. *American Journal of Occupational Therapy, 57*(5), 534–541.

Sforza, T., Lenhoff, H., & Lenhoff, S. (2006). *The strangest song: One father's quest to help his daughter find her voice*. Amherst, NY: Prometheus Books.

Shah, A., & Frith, S. (1983). An islet of ability in autistic children: A research note. *Journal of Child Psychology and Psychiatry, 24*(4), 613–620.

Shah, A., & Frith, U. (1993). Why do autistic individuals show superior performance on the block design task? *Journal of Child Psychology and Psychiatry, 34*(8), 1351–1364.

Shaw, P., Eckstrand, K., Sharp, W., Blumenthal, J., Lerch, J. P., Greenstein, D., Clasen, L., Evans, A., Giedd, J., & Rapoport, J. L. (2007, December 4). Attention-deficit/hyperactivity disorder is characterized by a delay in cortical maturation. *Proceedings of the National Academy of Sciences, 104*(49), 19649–19654.

Shaywitz, B. A., Fletcher, J. M., & Shaywitz, S. E. (1995, January 10). Defining and classifying learning disabilities and attention-deficit/hyperactivity disorder. *Journal of Child Neurology 10*(Suppl. 1), S50–S57.

Shaywitz, B. A., & Shaywitz, S. E. (2009). Brain imaging in studies of reading and dyslexia. *In Encyclopedia of Language and Literacy Development* (pp. 1–6). London, Ontario: Canadian Language and Literacy Research Network. Retrieved from http://www.literacyencyclopedia.ca/pdfs/topic/php?topId=281

Shaywitz, S. (n.d.) A conversation with Sally Shaywitz. Retrieved from Great Schools at http://www.greatschools.org/special-education/LD-ADHD/836-a-conversation-with-sally-shaywitz-m-d-author-of-overcoming-dyslexia.gs

Shaywitz, S. (2008, March/April). Slow readers, creative thinkers: Gift will spur dyslexia studies. *Medicine@Yale Newsletter, 4*(1). Retrieved from http://info.med.yale.edu/ysm/medicineatyale/v4i1_mar_april_2008/thinkers.html

Simeonova, D. I., Chang, K. D., Strong, C., & Ketter, T. A. (2005, November). Creativity in familial bipolar disorder. *Journal of Psychiatric Research, 39*(6), 623–631.

Sinclair, J. (1993). Don't mourn for us. *Our Voice, 1*(3). Retrieved from http://www.autreat.com/dont_mourn.html

Singer, J. (1999). Why can't you be normal for once in your life? In M. Corker & S. French (Eds.), *Disability discourse*. Buckingham, United Kingdom: Open University Press.

Skotko, B. G., Levine, S. P., & Goldstein, R. (2011). Self-perceptions from people with Down syndrome. *American Journal of Medical Genetics, Part A, 155*(10), 2360–2369.

Slingerland, B. H. (1996). *A multi-sensory approach to language arts for specific language disability children* (rev. ed.). Cambridge, MA: Educators Publishing Service.

Smith, P., & O'Brien, J. (2007, October). Have we made any progress? Including students with intellectual disabilities in regular education classrooms. *Intellectual and Developmental Disabilities, 45*(5), 297–309.

Special Olympics. (2005). *Changing attitudes, changing the world: Changing lives through sport: A study of youth attitudes about intellectual disabilities*. Retrieved from http://www.specialolympics.org/uploadedFiles/LandingPage/WhatWeDo/Research_Studies_Desciption_Pages/Policy_paper_youth_attitudes.pdf

Spencer, V. G., & Balboni, G. (2003). Can students with mental retardation teach their peers? *Education and Training in Developmental Disabilities, 38*(1), 32–61.

Steinfeld, E., & Maisel, J. (2012). *Universal design: Creating inclusive environments*. Hoboken, NJ: Wiley.

Stuart, S. K. (2003, February). Choice or chance: Career development and girls with emotional or behavioral disorders. *Behavioral Disorders, 28*(2), 150–161.

Suter, J. C., & Bruns, E. J. (2009). Effectiveness of the wraparound process for children with emotional and behavioral disorders: A meta-analysis. *Clinical Child and Family Psychology Review, 12*(4), 336–351.

Sutherland, K. S., & Snyder, A. (2007, Summer). Effects of reciprocal peer tutoring and self-graphing on reading fluency and classroom behavior of middle school students with emotional or behavioral disorders. *Journal of Emotional and Behavioral Disorders, 15*(2), 103–118.

Temple, E., Deutsch, G. K., Poldrack, R. A., Miller, S. L., Tallal, P., Merzenich, M. M., & Gabrieli, J. D. E. (2003, March 4). Neural deficits in children with dyslexia ameliorated by behavioral remediation: Evidence from functional MRI. *Proceedings of the National Academy of Science, 100*(5), 2860–2865.

The Arc. (2011, June). *Still in the shadows with their future uncertain: A report on family and individual needs for disability supports (FINDS), 2011*. Washington, DC: Author.

Tomlinson, C. A. (2004). *How to differentiate instruction in mixed ability classrooms.* Alexandria, VA: ASCD.

Tomlinson, C. A., & Imbeau, M. B. (2010). *Leading and managing a differentiated classroom.* Alexandria, VA: ASCD.

Torrance, E. P. (1974). *The Torrance tests of creative thinking.* New York: Scholastic Testing Service.

Treffert, D. (2009, May). The savant syndrome: An extraordinary condition. A synopsis: past, present, and future. *Philosophical Transactions of the Royal Society, B, Biological Sciences, 364*(1522), 1351–1357.

U.S. Department of Education, National Center for Education Statistics. (2011). *Digest of education statistics, 2010.* Retrieved from http://nces.ed.gov/fastfacts/display.asp?id=64

Visu-Petra, L., Benga, O., Tincas, I., & Miclea, M. (2007, December). Visual-spatial processing in children and adolescents with Down's syndrome: A computerized assessment of memory skills. *Journal of Intellectual Disability Research, 51*(12), 942–952.

Wang, P. P. (1996, December). Neuropsychological profile of Down syndrome: Cognitive skills and brain morphology. *Mental Retardation and Developmental Disabilities Research Reviews, 2,* 102–108.

Warren, C. (2008, July 1). Coudl this be teh sercet to sussecc? *American Way.* Retrieved from http://www.americanwaymag.com/dyslexia-hunt-lowry-sally-shaywitz-julie-logan

Wehmeyer, M. L., & Field, S. L. (2007). *Self-determination: Instructional and assessment strategies.* Thousand Oaks, CA: Corwin Press.

Weinstein, R. S. (2004). *Reaching higher: The power of expectations in schooling.* Cambridge, MA: Harvard University Press.

West, T. G. (1991). *In the mind's eye: Visual thinkers, gifted people with learning difficulties, computer images, and the ironies of creativity.* New York: Prometheus Books.

White, H. A., & Shaw, P. (2011, April). Creative style and achievement in adults with attention deficit/hyperactivity disorder. *Journal of Personality and Individual Differences, 5*(5), 673–677.

Williams, G. J., Kitchener, G., Press, L. J., Scheiman, M. M., & Steele, G. T. (2004, November). The use of tinted lenses and colored overlays for the treatment of dyslexia and other related reading and learning disorders. *Optometry: Journal of the American Optometric Association, 75*(11), 720–722.

Winter-Messiers, M. A. (2007, May/June). From tarantulas to toilet brushes: Understanding the special interest areas of children and youth with Asperger syndrome. *Remedial and Special Education, 28*(3), 140–152.

Wuang, Y. P., Chiang, C. S., Su, C. Y., & Wang, C. C. (2011, January/February). Effectiveness of virtual reality using Wii gaming technology in children with Down syndrome. *Research in Developmental Disabilities, 32*(1), 312–321.

Zax, D. (2011, September 7). A dancing robot that could help the autistic. *Technology Review.* Retrieved from http://www.technologyreview.com/blog/helloworld/27139/?p1=blogs

Zentall, S. S., (2005). Theory and evidence-based strategies for children with attentional problems. *Psychology in the Schools, 42*(8), 821–836.

Zhang, J., & Wheeler, J. J. (2011). A meta-analysis of peer-mediated interventions for young children with autism spectrum disorders. *Education and Training in Autism and Developmental Disabilities, 46*(1), 62–77.

Index

The letter *f* following a page number denotes a figure, and positive niche construction components have been capitalized for easy reference.

About the Author

 **Thomas Armstrong** has been an educator for the past 40 years. He worked for several years as a special education teacher in the United States and Canada, developed courses in human development for colleges and universities in the San Francisco Bay area, and served as an educational consultant for schools in New York State. For the past 26 years, he has been an author, keynote speaker, and workshop leader in 43 states and 19 countries.

Armstrong is the author of 15 books, including six with ASCD: *Multiple Intelligences in the Classroom*, 3rd edition, *ADD/ADHD Alternatives in the Classroom*, *Awakening Genius in the Classroom*, *The Multiple Intelligences of Reading and Writing*, *The Best Schools*, and *Neurodiversity in the Classroom*. His other books include *7 Kinds of Smart, In Their Own Way, The Myth of the A.D.D. Child, The Human Odyssey*, and *The Power of Neurodiversity*. His books have been translated into 26 languages, including Chinese, Hebrew, Russian, Spanish, and Portuguese. He has also written for *Family Circle, Ladies' Home Journal, Parenting*, and many other periodicals and journals in the United States and abroad.

Armstrong's clients have included the Children's Television Workshop (the creators of *Sesame Street*), the Bureau of Indian Affairs, the European Council of International Schools, the Republic of Singapore, and several state departments of education. He lives in Sonoma County, California, in a pink Victorian with his wife and two Shih Tzu dogs. You can reach the author by mail at P.O. Box 548, Cloverdale, CA 95425; by phone at 707-894-4646 (land line) or 707-328-2659 (cell); by fax at 707-894-4474; or by e-mail at thomas@thomasarmstrong.com. His website and blog are at www.thomasarmstrong.com.

Related ASCD Resources: Inclusion

At the time of publication, the following ASCD resources were available (ASCD stock numbers appear in parentheses). For up-to-date information about ASCD resources, go to www.ascd.org. You can search the complete archives of *Educational Leadership* at http://www.ascd.org/el.

ASCD EDge Group

Exchange ideas and connect with other educators interested in inclusion on the social networking site ASCD EDge™ at http://ascdedge.ascd.org/.

Online Courses

Inclusion: The Basics, 2nd Edition (#PD11OC121)
Inclusion: Implementing Strategies, 2nd Edition (#PD11OC122)

Print Products

Educational Leadership (February 2007): Improving Instruction for Students with Learning Needs (#107030)
Brain-Friendly Strategies for the Inclusion Classroom by Judy Willis (#107040)
Creating an Inclusive School, 2nd Edition by Richard Villa and Jacqueline S. Thousand (#105019)
Inclusive Schools in Action: Making Differences Ordinary by James McLeskey and Nancy L. Waldron (#100210)

DVDs

Teaching Students with Learning Disabilities in the Regular Classroom (with online facilitator's guide; #602084)

THE WHOLE CHILD The Whole Child Initiative helps schools and communities create learning environments that allow students to be healthy, safe, engaged, supported, and challenged. To learn more about other books and resources that relate to the whole child, visit www.wholechildeducation.org.

For more information: send e-mail to member@ascd.org; call 1-800-933-2723 or 703-578-9600, press 2; send a fax to 703-575-5400; or write to Information Services, ASCD, 1703 N. Beauregard St., Alexandria, VA 22311-1714 USA.